MEETINGHIM
BENETH PETERS JONES

journey**forth**®

Greenville, South Carolina

Library of Congress Cataloging-in-Publication Data

Jones, Beneth Peters, 1937
  Meeting Him / Beneth Peters Jones.
     p. cm.
  Summary: "A women's study of the Bible scenes in which Jesus had
dealings with women" Provided by publisher.
  ISBN 978 1 60682 022 3 (pbk. : alk. paper)
  1. Women in the Bible. 2. Jesus Christ Friends and associates. I. Title.
BS2445.J66 2009
226.09'2082 dc22

                                    2009015728

Study Guide Questions: Suzette Jordan
Cover Photo Credits: Craig Oesterling

The fact that materials produced by other publishers may be referred
to in this volume does not constitute an endorsement of the content or
theological position of materials produced by such publishers.

All Scripture is quoted from the Authorized King James Version.

Meeting Him

Design by Nick Ng
Page layout by Michael Boone

© 2010 by BJU Press
Greenville, South Carolina 29614
JourneyForth Books is a division of BJU Press

Printed in the United States of America

ISBN 978-1-60682-022-3
15   14   13   12   11   10   9   8   7   6   5   4   3   2

In grateful memory of Sherri, Billie, and Carolyn, dear friends who beautifully demonstrated having met Jesus Christ. Each one's heart attachment to Him inspired those of us privileged to walk beside them.

CONTENTS

THERE THEY ARE—
BUT WHY?

The New Testament opens in a way that may appear less than exciting. Yet God chose to bridge His Testaments with a genealogy. Genealogical lists, such as that found in Matthew 1, certainly don't seem a huge spiritual blessing. Interest in such lists is pretty much limited to folks who make a business or hobby of tracing family roots. Nevertheless, all of us can recognize practical aspects of recorded lineages. They can provide clues to physical or mental health puzzles or establish inheritance legalities. But why has God preserved detailed, lengthy generational lists? In the first place, such records helped maintain Israel's tribal identities through the centuries. More importantly, they catalog and connect the mortal threads through which Jehovah's promised Messiah took on human flesh.

In the general sense, then, Bible genealogies remind us of God's faithfulness through preceding generations and His focus upon individuals. But there is also a specific blessing for you and me, the Lord's female children. The recorded line as seen in Matthew is not just a lengthy collection of "begats." Interspersed among the male forebears of Jesus are four women. And what women they were: Tamar . . . Rahab . . . Ruth . . . and Bathsheba. Those who are familiar with the Bible immediately recognize their names. All those women would seem to be disqualified because of roots or reputation, and we marvel that they were allowed in the human bloodline of Jesus. But in each case the disqualifying stains of sin were purged and the sinner made pure by the marvelous grace of the Lord God Jehovah. Thus Tamar the incestuous, Rahab the prostitute, Ruth the Moabite, and Bathsheba the adulteress appear in the lineage. What a potent reminder—right at the opening of the New Testament—that no one is beyond God's ability to save or beneath His ability to use.

Jehovah's special tenderness toward women indicated in the genealogical record carries through into the New Testament narrative, where we see Jesus—God in flesh—interacting with women.

As a Christian woman reading the Gospels, I've naturally been magnetized by the moments in Jesus' life when He crossed paths with women. Before His coming to earth, women generally enjoyed little respect, valuation, or opportunity. At best they were second-class citizens. God Incarnate accorded them a new level of recognition. By example He taught that women are important as individuals and that their contribution is valuable. He repeatedly ignored or rebuked those who would have turned His attention to "more important" things. Further, He strengthened the divine injunction against men's sexual misuse of women by proclaiming that a lustful look was sinful. He also spoke against the male-serving easy divorce practices that had been adopted by the Jews.

One of the most powerful, evident, and unusual characteristics of the Bible is its succinctness. However, such brevity demands three things of a Bible reader who wants to glean richly from the text: a slow and careful reading of the passage(s), deeply pondering the words themselves and imaginatively projecting oneself into the recorded situations. When studying individuals who appear in Scripture, I use the Bible page like a doorway through which I walk to come up close to the individual, to see and sense the person's reality. When the subject takes on the resulting extra dimension of acquaintanceship, blessings from that life multiply exponentially.

The challenge to undertake this particular writing project came from the closing words in John's Gospel:

> And there are also many other things which Jesus did, the which, if they should be written every one, I suppose that even the world itself could not contain the books that should be written. (21:25)

Considering such wealth of unrecorded situations, meetings, healings, and so forth, as "the beloved disciple" indicates, why did God select the relative few we find in the Bible's pages? He is the God of order and purpose. He does nothing offhandedly. It seems obvious, therefore, that individuals and incidents He presents were chosen in order to communicate an important part of His message. Yet we—personally—seldom take the time or make the effort to immerse ourselves sufficiently in Scripture's characters and incidents to absorb their meaning.

There were many times, places, and situations in which women came to Jesus' attention. Each of those individuals experienced something special in meeting Him. My purpose is to highlight each woman—in chronological order—whose personal interaction with Jesus Christ is recorded.

> For whatsoever things were written aforetime were written for our learning, that we through patience and comfort of the scriptures might have hope. (Rom. 15:4)

Although Paul's commendation referred to Old Testament Scriptures, the same certainly extends to the New Testament writings.

I believe that the collected narratives involving women are meant to present an extensive—and perhaps even complete—diorama of feminine characteristics, experiences, and needs, to reflect our own personal relationship with Jesus Christ. Although the bodies of the women Jesus met here on earth turned to dust long ago, their stories live on and speak to us in the twenty-first century.

The following pages present the Bible scenes in which Jesus had dealings with women. In each we will follow the read-ponder-project approach, developing the written sketch into a fuller picture. My purpose is simply to encourage practical, personal application. This writing is not meant as scholarly research; I'm not trying to prove anything or impress anyone. Rather, I yearn to treat each woman in such a way that we meet her on a human level. It is on that level—person to person and heart to heart—that we best learn from one another, isn't it?

My searching through the clues may or may not produce accurate portraits. But perhaps at least enough will be seen in each woman that we can move with her as she comes face to face with the Lord Jesus Christ. I'm praying diligently to that end. May we examine the portraits with a questing heart so that in *Meeting Him* with these women we may be challenged and changed for His glory.

In His love—and mine,
Beneth

Chapter 1
MARY, MOTHER OF JESUS

Obviously, Mary was the very first woman Jesus "met." His relationship with her, from before His birth through His death and resurrection, meant tremendous, lifelong spiritual growth for her.

While we must guard against the numberless inferences drawn from and myths grown up around Mary, we also should rightly honor one whom God honors in His Word.

Each of us can emulate Mary's moral purity, empathize with her maternal suffering, and be encouraged by our shared humanity. But the real Mary as presented in Scripture would not recognize herself as religion has distorted her; she would, rather, abhor it all. A mere human being, she—like each of us other ordinary women—was a sinner who depended for salvation upon the shed blood of Jesus Christ. Initially she was chosen to bear the physical body of the baby Jesus, but eventually she chose to believe in Him as the Christ—Savior of all mankind including herself. Hers was a unique physical bond with Him, but it did not in any way bestow upon her spiritual uniqueness or elevation into the heavenlies.

Of the four Gospels, only Luke puts any focus upon Mary. He alone provides narrative color and detail. With his physician's interest in that which is human, he sketchily presents Mary's portrait. What lies beyond the charcoal strokes—her individual dimensions and color? Luke first locates Mary geographically: she lived in Nazareth, a city in Galilee. Jews scorned the idea of their Messiah originating in Nazareth: people in Judea looked down upon Galileans as inferior in their Jewishness as well as generally crude and countrified. Moreover, the city of Nazareth was particularly despised. "And Nathaniel said unto [Philip], Can there any good thing come out of Nazareth?" (John 1:46).

Thus in the very beginning of Mary's story, we're reminded that God's thoughts and ways are unlike ours: from the first moments of the promised incarnation, His love is shown shed abroad to unnoteworthy regions and people.

The Scripture narrative begins by showing that Mary was not exclusive in experiencing a miracle. Luke connects the angel's annunciation to her with another important pregnancy: that of Elisabeth, Mary's cousin. Formerly barren and advanced in age, Elisabeth was six months along in carrying Jesus' forerunner, who would become known as John the Baptist. Jesus would later state that among those born of women there was none greater than John.

This, then, is how the spotlight of history first shone upon a simple peasant girl named Mary:

> And in the sixth month the angel Gabriel was sent from God unto a city of Galilee, named Nazareth, to a virgin espoused to a man whose name was Joseph, of the house of David; and the virgin's name was Mary. (Luke 1:26–27)

Mary was probably in her early teens, since girls of that time married young. God didn't see fit to record her physical age or any

other identifying detail, but notice that He pointed out a prime
fact of her spiritual identity: she was a virgin. Although she'd
entered into the covenant relationship of betrothal to Joseph, she
was obedient to God's law and was remaining sexually pure prior
to their marriage.

> And the angel came in unto her, and said, Hail, thou that art
> highly favoured, the Lord is with thee: blessed art thou among
> women. (Luke 1:28)

Artists and our own imaginations make that moment highly
dramatic, with blazing light and an otherworldly being. But I
wonder. Mary wasn't overpoweringly shocked or awed by the
angel's appearance; rather, her reaction can be better described as
positive and thoughtful:

> And when she saw him, she was troubled at his saying, and cast
> in her mind what manner of salutation this should be. (1:29)

Very likely Gabriel's physical appearance was little out of the
ordinary. But what he had to say certainly was! Such a salutation
to a young peasant girl was bewildering. Perhaps even the "cast-
ing in her mind" was a questioning of the stranger's own mental
capacity. Put yourself in Mary's place: the sudden appearance of
an unknown person speaking such a strange greeting would make
you wonder if the fellow had escaped from a padded cell, wouldn't
it? But of course the words of address were just the beginning.
Gabriel went on to make his momentous pronouncement.

> Fear not, Mary: for thou hast found favour with God. And,
> behold, thou shalt conceive in thy womb, and bring forth a son,
> and shalt call his name JESUS. He shall be great, and shall
> be called the Son of the Highest: and the Lord God shall give
> unto him the throne of his father David: and he shall reign over

the house of Jacob for ever; and of his kingdom there shall be no end. (1:30–33)

Notice the angel—this total stranger—called her by name and immediately pulled her mind from puzzling over him, the messenger, to focus upon God and His message. She was to be a participant in Jehovah's central act within all human history.

Mary didn't question the truth of Gabriel's pronouncement. Her understanding was of course limited to the natural world. But her instant, simple acceptance of the stated happening is absolutely amazing. Her response simply harks back to that important character facet mentioned earlier: her virginity. In view of her physical purity she asked, "How shall this be, seeing I know not a man?" (1:34).

She doesn't sound like a typical young teenage girl. No wonder she had found favor in God's sight! I recall an incident in our daughter Roxane's childhood. One afternoon while her younger brothers napped, she was playing quietly with dolls in her bedroom. As I passed her door, she was dramatizing Gabriel's announcement to Mary:

Gabriel: Don't be afraid, Mary. You're going to have a baby. He'll be called Jesus.

Mary: How? I don't have a husband.

Gabriel: I don't care.

Mary: Then I don't care either.

That's a pretty accurate summation of the exchange, isn't it? Mary simply accepted what the angel said and believed it.

Gabriel then called upon Mary to move beyond her concern about the natural to recognize the supernatural: "The Holy Ghost shall come upon thee, and the power of the Highest shall overshadow thee: therefore also that holy thing which shall be born of thee shall be called the Son of God" (1:35).

God's overshadowing would enable her body to be the conduit whereby deity would become humanity, eternality would constrict itself into time, and omnipotence would become infant helplessness. Those who are knowledgeable in the language of Scripture point out that the word translated "overshadow" is the same used in the Old Testament to describe God's dwelling within the holy of holies.

Just as Scripture prefaces Gabriel's announcement to Mary with Elisabeth's miraculous pregnancy, so too Gabriel turned the girl's attention from her own promised miracle to Elisabeth's, which was already in progress: "And, behold, thy cousin Elisabeth, she hath also conceived a son in her old age: and this is the sixth month with her, who was called barren" (1:36).

Why such a quick transition to the revelation of Elisabeth's pregnancy? Was it lest Mary feel exclusive in God's special intervention and blessing? Was it to point Mary toward someone who could "come alongside" her rather than stand in disbelief and disdain? Whatever was intended in the horizontal sense, the angel clearly stated the vertical focus: "For with God nothing shall be impossible" (1:37).

The important point was not either woman or her experience, but God's power. Then Mary spoke briefly again—not a question but the simple, straightforward response of her yielded heart— "Behold, the handmaid of the Lord; be it unto me according to thy word" (1:38).

You and I have probably read this passage so often that we glance at the words, hurrying on to Mary's visit with Elisabeth. But the girl's fourteen words—even perhaps spoken when she was fourteen—contain libraries of faith and commitment.

Imagine yourself in Mary's place. A stranger has approached you. He has called you by name! He has announced that you are a special focus of Jehovah's attention. He has left you agape by telling you that, as a sexually pure girl, you are going to become pregnant via a miracle. Wouldn't the angel's message explode like a bomb in your mind and heart? Emotional fragments must surely have rushed into the girl's consciousness—the disbelief of others, the social stigma, the possible shattered relationships. But the heavenly visitor didn't address the inevitable fallout at all.

Whatever her emotional and mental quandary, Mary didn't question. She didn't argue. She didn't hesitate, asking for time to think things through. She yielded instantly and totally, identifying herself as the lowest of female servants, a handmaid—one who had no rights but was entirely controlled by, responsible to, and at the disposal of those she served. Mary presented herself unreservedly for the performance of God's will. "And the angel departed from her" (1:38*b*).

What a brief visitation, what a strange messenger, and how astounding the news delivered that day! Considering Mary in the aftermath of those moments, I'm again amazed at the girl's character. There is no indication that she fainted from overwrought emotions, argued against the reality of the experience, or reconsidered her acceptance and commitment.

After she had responded in such immediate compliance to the angel's message, she went to visit her cousin. The angel's revelation of Elisabeth's pregnancy not only underlined God's miracle-working power but it also opened a door through which Mary could move for encouragement and help. "And Mary arose in those days, and went into the hill country with haste, into a city of Judah; and entered into the house of Zacharias, and saluted Elisabeth" (1:39–40).

Regardless of how promptly Mary had accepted the unique role assigned to her by God, her humanity demanded some time for withdrawal and contemplation. How graciously the Lord had supplied someone to reach out to her in her time of need. The two women, one old and one young, together had entered a universe apart from the realm of ordinary human experience. Both a special bond of understanding and the hierarchy of their relationship come through to us in Elisabeth's words of greeting to Mary:

> Blessed art thou among women, and blessed is the fruit of thy womb. And whence is this to me, that the mother of my Lord should come to me? For, lo, as soon as the voice of thy salutation sounded in mine ears, the babe leaped in my womb for joy. And blessed is she that believed: for there shall be a performance of those things which were told her from the Lord. (1:42*b*–45)

Notice that Elisabeth's greeting parallels and underlines that of the angel: "Blessed art thou among women." A subtle but strategic reality can be found in that twice-spoken salutation: Mary was not honored by God *above* all other women but *among* them. That draws an enormously important boundary beyond which we must not go in honoring Mary. Idolizing her lies outside those bounds—it is distortion and deception.

Surely in terms of her human womanhood Mary must have experienced significant emotional comfort as she heard Elisabeth's confirmation of the angelic message. And then, warmed by the bond of the special female relationship with her cousin, Mary was free to let pour from her heart the rapture she'd kept within until that moment.

> My soul doth magnify the Lord, and my spirit hath rejoiced in God my Saviour. For he hath regarded the low estate of his handmaiden: for, behold, from henceforth all generations shall call me blessed. For he that is mighty hath done to me great things: and holy is his name. And his mercy is on them that fear him from generation to generation. He hath showed

strength with his arm; he hath scattered the proud in the imagination of their hearts. He hath put down the mighty from their seats, and exalted them of low degree. He hath filled the hungry with good things; and the rich he hath sent empty away. He hath holpen his servant Israel, in remembrance of his mercy. As he spake to our fathers, to Abraham, and to his seed for ever. (1:46*b*–55)

This Magnificat can be sweetly instructive to each of us these many centuries after it came from Mary's lips. The beautiful verbal magnification is not of Mary herself at all, but of her God. Acknowledging His greatness was the motivation for her rapturous expression. It is not just an emotional burbling, but rich evidence of Mary's Scripture knowledge. It's as if her soul had reached such a high plane of praise that only the language of heaven itself could express it. She didn't focus upon her personal blessing of the moment, but upon God's character, His power, and His faithfulness throughout the ages.

The time Elisabeth and Mary spent together must have been rich with encouragement for both of them. Their drawing together in those days doubtless transcended the ordinary positives of feminine friendship as well as the bond of family relationships: "And Mary abode with her about three months, and returned to her own house" (1:56).

We're not told what went on between the two women during those three months, but it's interesting to speculate. Mary was in the beginning of her pregnancy and Elisabeth in the final phase of hers. Elisabeth might naturally have helped Mary in terms of accommodating her morning sickness and informing and preparing her for the gestational months still to come. But the tone set in their moment of greeting indicates that there was greater emphasis upon and fuller delight in things of the spirit.

Elisabeth's husband, Zacharias, was a priest. Besides his years of exemplary priestly service, he had also recently experienced the angelic visitation and God's miraculous gift of fertility. Surely the faithful old fellow, though mute by Gabriel's decree, would have pointed his wife and her visiting cousin to Scripture, leading them away from any threatened emotionalism to the settled reality of the Word's prophecy.

Even the home atmosphere of Elisabeth and Zacharias, who had walked, together, with God for many years, must have comforted the teenage girl upon whom such an immeasurable, shaking reality had come.

Mary stayed with Elisabeth three months. Surely that period of time in which the women were together was a significant part of God's plan for both of them. By the end of it (when her pregnancy would have begun to show in her body), we can hope and assume that Mary returned to Nazareth equipped with whatever human strengthening she had needed as she began to face the misunderstanding, suspicions, scorn, gossip, ridicule, and lifelong challenges that awaited her.

Back in Nazareth, Mary had cause to rejoice in Joseph's God-obedient acceptance of her as pure and worthy of becoming his wife. His wonderful, quiet response of belief against all human logic and comprehension marks the simple carpenter as a fitting stepfather for the Son of God. Little is said of Joseph in Scripture, but the few words accorded him reveal enormous spiritual faith and human character.

Nothing more is shown us of Mary until she reached the cattle stall in Bethlehem six months later. God's precise working with regard to time and place is evident in that stable setting. The demanded taxation actually had been decreed by Caesar Augustus four years earlier; but protests by the Jews and slow processing by the Roman government throughout its conquered regions resulted in delay—"delay" that found Mary and Joseph in Bethlehem. Times, seasons, governments, and individuals were directed by God's sovereign will in order that prophecy might be fulfilled:

> But thou, Bethlehem Ephratah, though thou be little among the thousands of Judah, yet out of thee shall he come forth unto me that is to be ruler in Israel; whose goings forth have been from of old, from everlasting. (Mic. 5:2)

There birth pangs came upon Mary, demanding their stay be extended in the little town whose name means "House of Bread." It was "the fulness of time"—time for the Bread of heaven to appear.

> And it came to pass in those days, that there went out a decree from Caesar Augustus, that all the world should be taxed. . . . And all went to be taxed, every one into his own city. And Joseph also went up from Galilee, out of the city of Nazareth, into Judea, unto the city of David, which is called Bethlehem; (because he was of the house and lineage of David:) to be taxed with Mary his espoused wife, being great with child. And so it was, that, while they were there, the days were accomplished that she should be delivered. And she brought forth her first-born son, and wrapped him in swaddling clothes, and laid him in a manger; because there was no room for them in the inn. (Luke 2:1–7)

That extremely humble, highly unusual place of His appearance on earth is given, but her experience in delivering the babe is not. Nor would Mary desire to pull focus toward herself and away from that One newly stepped from eternity into time. Instead . . . "Mary kept all these things, and pondered them in her heart" (Luke 2:19).

The new mother's preference for privacy was disturbed by
the shepherds who came to the stable birthplace in response to the
angels' radiant proclamation: "Unto you is born this day in the city
of David a Saviour, which is Christ the Lord" (Luke 2:11).

Not only did rough, humble shepherds make worshipful visits
to her child but wealthy, exotic foreign dignitaries later came as
well. Joseph and Mary's quiet world was transformed as God
allowed others to know of His incarnation. So she pondered—
such wondrous things were said of her baby—how were they to
play out in years ahead? How could she—how could any mortal
woman—hope to fulfill the role of mother to Him Who was the
eternal, omniscient God? It must surely be she the human mother
who would grow and learn.

Had Mary been the queenly, sinless woman caricatured to the
world by Catholicism, all the earlier scenes would have played far
differently. A "sinless" Mary might have chided Gabriel, "Aha—
it's about time you found me. As queen-of-heaven-to-be, I'm of
course ready to take the stage here. My son and I will do the salvation bit hand in hand." She would have vied for visitors' attention,
relishing every opportunity to highlight her role. She might even
have begun a lecture tour, presenting a nine-point program for
currying Jehovah's favor.

Mary and Joseph faithfully provided a normal Jewish babyhood for Jesus, thereby cooperating with Jehovah's intention that
from the outset His Son would not flout or destroy the law but
would fulfill it.

> And when eight days were accomplished for the circumcising
> of the child, his name was called JESUS, which was so named
> of the angel before he was conceived in the womb. And when
> the days of her purification according to the law of Moses were
> accomplished, they brought him to Jerusalem, to present him to

the Lord . . . and to offer a sacrifice according to that which is
said in the law of the Lord, a pair of turtledoves, or two young
pigeons. (Luke 2:21–22, 24)

In that moment of His temple dedication with their sacrificial
offering of birds, the behavior and words of two aged servants of
the Lord, Simeon and Anna, added to Mary's ponderings. Stand
with her; watch and listen.

And, behold, there was a man in Jerusalem, whose name was
Simeon; and the same man was just and devout, waiting for the
consolation of Israel: and the Holy Ghost was upon him. And
it was revealed unto him by the Holy Ghost, that he should not
see death, before he had seen the Lord's Christ. And he came
by the Spirit into the temple: and when the parents brought in
the child Jesus, to do for him after the custom of the law, then
took he him up in his arms, and blessed God, and said, Lord,
now lettest thou thy servant depart in peace, according to thy
word: for mine eyes have seen thy salvation. (Luke 2:25–30)

Then Jesus was folded back into the privacy of His own family. There was a dramatic interlude as they fled to Egypt to escape
Herod's murderous wrath, but God foiled that first attempt to kill
Jesus. Matthew 2 gives us an overview of His protective intervention. In general, though, Jesus' days of youth were unexceptional.

How Mary must have treasured what we call the "silent years"
of Jesus' boyhood! How sweet must have been the joys of watching Him, along with His siblings, grow as individuals, navigate
the various stages from babyhood through adolescence, and relate
to one another in the family. How precious must have been the
quietness and normalcy of life in Nazareth supported by Joseph's
carpentry.

Then came a Passover celebration that shook the family's
sense of normalcy. Jesus was twelve years old, and the journey to

Jerusalem for Passover observance would have been expected to fit the annual family pattern. But in that final year before He entered His teens, Jesus gave evidence of transition that was far more than mere puberty. Their family experienced the crowds, activities, and general bustle of Passover as usual until Mary, Joseph, their other children, and whatever relatives and friends accompanying them left Jerusalem for the return trip to Nazareth. But at the end of their first day on the road they missed Jesus. Rather than going home with His family as He'd done in prior years, Jesus had stayed behind. For three long days they searched for Him. Imagine the parents' great unease as they, unsophisticated village people, went back into the maze of Jerusalem's unfamiliar streets; their questioning of acquaintances and strangers; their fear of what might have befallen Him. At last they found Him in the temple. Their unexceptional home life and relationships to that point had given them no reason to suspect His whereabouts; they were amazed to find Him in the temple. He hadn't stayed for typical, preteen reasons. He hadn't stayed to gawk. He hadn't taken up with a group of rowdy young acquaintances trying to liven up the somber temple atmosphere. He was with the religious leaders—mature and aged men who had spent their lives studying the Scripture scrolls and Jewish traditions. He was listening to them and drawing upon their knowledge by posing questions. He was comfortable among those learned individuals, but Joseph and Mary probably were intimidated by the group.

Whatever her embarrassment or unease in the face of the impressive assembly, Mary had endured too much worry in their searching to remain silent; she voiced her maternal concern: "Son, why hast thou thus dealt with us? behold, thy father and I have sought thee sorrowing" (2:48*b*). The answer He gave certainly was not anything she might have expected: "How is it that ye sought me? wist ye not that I must be about my Father's business?" (2:49*b*).

It seems Jesus purposely echoed the word *father* that Mary used to recall His earthly parents' attention to His true identity and purpose. Whether the reminder was effective or meaningless at the moment, Joseph and Mary concentrated on leaving Jerusalem and heading home again—this time with Jesus in tow. "And he went down with them, and came to Nazareth, and was subject unto them" (2:51*a*).

Until my most recent time spent in the passage, I had not seen anything significant in these words. But there is. Jesus had newly exercised His true spiritual self there among the theological minds in the temple. Too, He had taken a step beyond boyhood by independently choosing to linger in the temple. And He was at the age when Jewish youth began the ceremonial transition into manhood. Despite those naturally invigorating factors, Jesus surrendered Himself again to parental discipline.

Safely returned to Nazareth, life settled back into routine, and Jesus continued in normal growth and progress for one His age. However, Mary had been jolted from the warmth and familiarity of what had gone before. "But his mother kept all these sayings in her heart" (2:51*b*).

The scene of young Jesus with the religious elders in the temple and His words about His Father's business must have been burned into her mind to replay endlessly thereafter. Jesus left behind Him in Jerusalem's temple His atypical intelligence and Scripture knowledge, reverting to normal behavior and development. The Bible makes it clear that His growth through the teen years was neither otherworldly nor miraculous: "And Jesus increased in wisdom and stature, and in favour with God and man" (2:52).

Notice that His human development was multidimensional. The eternal mind of the Creator experienced the human mind's operation and expansion. Physically, too, He followed a normal growth pattern, transitioning from the body of a child into that of a young man. Even in His spiritual self there was growth—"increased in favour with God." And, finally, we're told there was social growth—"and [with] man." It's easy to see how an ordinary child needs to grow in all the ways mentioned, but our mind can't wrap itself around how God-in-flesh would do so. Evidently, everything in Jesus' preministry years was necessary for His full experiential identifying with us.

> For we have not an high priest which cannot be touched with
> the feeling of our infirmities; but was in all points tempted like
> as we are, yet without sin. (Heb. 4:15)

Then came Jesus' time to begin public ministry. We're not told the exact nature of the transition, but it seems the wedding at Cana was part of it, and Mary was present when He performed that first miracle. The marriage ceremony occurred after He had been recognized and baptized by John the Baptist and after He had called some to be His disciples: "And the third day there was a marriage in Cana of Galilee; and the mother of Jesus was there: and both Jesus was called, and his disciples, to the marriage" (John 2:1–2).

The wedding in Cana evidently involved relatives or family friends. Thus, the shortfall of provisions would have aroused Mary's sympathetic desire to help. When the supply of wine ran out, Mary went to Jesus and told Him of it. I've always wondered why she approached Him at all. Was it just out of concern that the host family not be embarrassed? Had Jesus through the years shown Himself to be naturally resourceful and imaginative in moments of minor crises? Since Joseph, apparently, had died, was it just reflexive for Mary to appeal to her oldest son for assistance? Had the hostess demonstrated such near panic that Mary felt compelled to enlist masculine logic and practicality? Did she simply wish for their family to contribute in the practical sense? Whatever moved her to approach Jesus, she felt confident of His help—though I doubt she expected miraculous intervention for such a mundane situation. His verbal response to her request seems abrupt and unfeeling: "Woman, what have I to do with thee? mine hour is not yet come" (2:4*b*).

Mary likely was as puzzled by Jesus' words as you and I are. But as we look into the incident today, we can bring the light of subsequent happenings to bear.

"Woman." He didn't call her "Mother." Did that very first word in His response indicate His moving beyond their private relationship into His public ministry? It would seem so, as the following question presents a further sense of separation from their personal bond: "What have I to do with thee? mine hour is not yet come" (2:4*b*).

She had appealed to Him for action, for provision in the practical, everyday sense. But from that time on His provision would be spiritual and eternal.

Mary wasn't crushed by Jesus' response; she didn't go into a snit, interpreting His words as disrespectful or cruel—hence neither should we think them so. The tone in which He likely spoke the words, her knowledge of Him through their special bond, and her years-long spiritual contemplation held her steady. She turned to those who were standing near and told them to do whatever He said. And there in her sight He wrought the first of the many miracles that would mark His earthly ministry and proclaim His true identity.

And there were set there six waterpots of stone, after the manner of the purifying of the Jews, containing two or three firkins
apiece. Jesus saith unto them, Fill the waterpots with water.
And they filled them up to the brim. And he saith unto them,
Draw out now, and bear unto the governor of the feast. And
they bare it. When the ruler of the feast had tasted the water
that was made wine, and knew not whence it was: (but the
servants which drew the water knew;) the governor of the feast
called the bridegroom, and saith unto him, Every man at the
beginning doth set forth good wine; and when men have well
drunk, then that which is worse; but thou hast kept the good
wine until now. (John 2:6–10)

As hubbub began over the quality of the miracle wine, Mary
didn't charge forward, either to tell her part in the incident or to
garner attention and praise for "her boy."

Each of the waterpots contained twenty or thirty gallons:
Jesus' miraculous provision was unmistakably abundant. There-
upon, "celebration" certainly applied to the wedding there in
Cana. Jesus blessed the occasion with His physical presence and
touched it with His spiritual power. For the disciples, His turning
water to wine certified His identity. Mary, who had long known
Who He was, must have been thrilled and yet shaken to see open
manifestation of His divine power. "This beginning of miracles
did Jesus in Cana of Galilee, and manifested forth his glory; and
his disciples believed on him" (John 2:11).

The next scene in which we see Mary with Jesus she acted
quite differently than at the Cana wedding. Matthew 12:46–49
presents the incident.

While he yet talked to the people, behold, his mother and his
brethren stood without, desiring to speak with him. Then one
said unto him, Behold, thy mother and thy brethren stand

without, desiring to speak with thee. But he answered and said
unto him that told him, Who is my mother? and who are my
brethren? And he stretched forth his hand toward his disciples,
and said, Behold my mother and my brethren!

By that point Jesus was wholly occupied with His active
ministry. Preceding chapters give us places He visited, sermons
He preached, and opposition He confronted. Such intense ministry involvement may have been the magnet bringing His "family
delegation" to visit. Coming unified as they did, their purpose can
be deduced: they desired their beloved son and brother to exercise
discretion. Doubtless they had followed His itinerary in considerable detail as reports came back to them from the many places
He visited. His unique proclamations and His incontrovertible
miracles were the subject of reports, rumors, and wildly divergent
opinions throughout the entire region.

Jesus' full-schedule pressures would have made His family members naturally concerned for His well-being. There may
have been something else inherent in the family's appeal: Jesus'
responsibility, as firstborn, to be more active in providing for them.
Too, in their love they must have yearned for Him to pull back on
His activities rather than exacerbate the ever-mounting religious
enmity.

It was not that Jesus rejected the natural concerns shown by
His family, nor that He repudiated them. But He had moved
beyond earthly ties to unfettered involvement in His Father's business. I wonder if perhaps His words to that effect, spoken those
years before when He was twelve, came to Mary's mind at the
time of this later event. She'd indeed kept, we're told, "all these
sayings in her heart." The attempted familial reining-in may have
been Mary's last close contact with Jesus. It would appear likely
from the Scripture narrative. Then through the following too-

short, too-swift months she could merely watch from afar as her beloved miracle child moved toward the unsuspected, shocking ultimate purpose for His coming to earth.

Next and finally, we see Mary at the cross. The scene appears in John 19:25–27.

> Now there stood by the cross of Jesus his mother and his mother's sister, Mary the wife of Cleophas, and Mary Magdalene.

The Bible's spotlight briefly swings to Mary immediately after the soldiers had gambled for Jesus' seamless outer garment. The prisoner had been stripped of His clothing and secured to the cross with iron spikes; then the soldiers were free to offset their grim duty with a bit of pleasantry: bidding against one another for the Nazarene's robe.

When you or I, as a mother, must stand by and watch one of our children in some type of suffering, our own pain sweeps in as if in pounding, foaming, towering waves. And our inability to help is a deadly undertow for our heart. With that relatively miniature experience in mind, move on now to Golgotha.

Even centuries after the event we cringe at the unspeakable horror of Jesus' hours on the cross. Medical research details crucifixion's torturous death, making any of us shudder in revulsion. Portrayals of Calvary in art and drama add impact through visual representation. But to see the bloody reality—just to stand among the gaping, hatred-spewing crowd . . . worse, to look upon such extreme suffering with followers' sorrow . . . but surely worst of all to watch with a mother's breaking heart—such dreadful immediacy lies beyond comprehension.

As she beheld Jesus' battered form hanging naked there, Mary must have revisited the days when she'd held Him secure and warm. She surely ached, too, as she relived the blessed days of His youth in their poor but peaceful home. But Calvary is not about Mary; it is about God—and you and me.

It's beautiful to see that there, at the end of Jesus' earthly life, He tenderly cared for the woman who had physically provided for its beginning:

> When Jesus therefore saw his mother, and the disciple standing by, whom he loved, he saith unto his mother, Woman, behold thy son! Then saith he to the disciple, Behold thy mother! And from that hour that disciple took her unto his own home. (19:26–27)

Amid the spiritually immense divine transaction of our redemption, Jesus demonstrated intimate humanity as He ensured care for His mother.

But why did Jesus give Mary to John? The Bible tells us that He had several brothers and sisters. They would seem to have been the natural ones to take up the care of their mother. Yet Jesus did not call upon that natural bond; apparently there was a greater spiritual factor operative in the situation. In the first place, belief in Jesus' identity as the Messiah came only tardily to His family members, as indicated in Matthew 13:57—"But Jesus said unto them, A prophet is not without honour, save in his own country, and in his own house."

And John 7:5 states it bluntly: "For neither did his brethren believe in him."

Second, Scripture refers to John several times as the beloved disciple or the disciple Jesus loved. He was in the three-member inner circle with whom the Lord shared special experiences and insights. Apparently the earthly closeness between Jesus and John indicated unique like-heartedness. So, although He was leaving His mother physically, He was providing the ongoing heart care that most closely echoed His own.

After Jesus' death, resurrection, and ascension, we're allowed to see Mary only once—when she was among the disciples in the upper room.

> These all continued with one accord in prayer and supplication, with the women, and Mary the mother of Jesus, and with his brethren. (Acts 1:14)

Mary is simply reported as being there among the others; she was neither isolated nor elevated. Throughout the years she had retained her status as an ordinary woman, one who had not risen above her common background or her humble social setting. The four Gospels mention her less frequently than they mention many of the disciples. Although she had been uniquely chosen by God as the human channel for His Son's coming to earth, she was not highlighted by Him for any other unusual life experience or focus of attention. As with every one of us, the channel is not important; only what God works through the channel is.

Mary was as limited in her comprehension of specifics in God's plan for Jesus to provide salvation as were any others around her. Her pondering, while it had an extra degree of biological rela- tionship in it, did not have any spark of divine enlightenment.

Mary disappears entirely from the Scripture scene after the fearful huddling of disciples in the upper room. Thus, she evi- dently held no privileged position among the increasing number of believers, played little or no part in the establishment of churches, and took no glory unto herself while the gospel of Jesus Christ turned the world upside down. Rather, her life in John's household allowed her a quiet fading into obscurity. In many respects that re- turn to the ordinary life of a commoner must have afforded Mary considerable relief.

What a shame to have false religion disturb her quietness and attempt to gaudily enthrone Mary as a co-savior; as "heaven's queen," the means of reaching and moving an otherwise aloof heart of God.

---

*M*EETING HIM WITH HER

There are many things in Mary's character and manner of life that can be of help to us.

First to strike me as a heart-lifting note is the unlikelihood of her place and person for God's choice. I immediately identify with both of those. In fact, who among us could possibly feel that in our self or our situation we are worthy of God's notice? We'd most likely have been entirely dismissed by human evaluation of potential. Isn't it amazing that the great creator God would have anything to do with us? It's not the worth of the clay, but the artistry, intention, and working of the Maker that determine the value of a vessel. Our wonderful Maker proclaims His inexplicable, sovereign working in Isaiah 43:25. "I, even I, am he that blotteth out thy transgressions for mine own sake, and will not remember thy sins."

It's also fitting to consider a matter that comes to us clearly in the Scripture text: Mary's virginity. Although as innately sinful as any other human being, Mary had not broken the seventh commandment. She conformed to the written Word before carrying and bearing the Living Word. Her physical purity had been foretold by Isaiah: "Therefore the Lord himself shall give you a sign; Behold, a virgin shall conceive, and bear a son, and shall call his name Immanuel" (Isa. 7:14).

I'm aware, from years of ministering to women of various ages, that a question may arise at this point. "But I'm not a virgin; can God use me?" Oh yes, my dear friend. God's choice of Mary was unique. Her physical purity was foreordained for fulfilling prophecy and making Jesus' conception unique.

If a girl or woman were to think she could not be saved or used because of impurity, in both instances she would be contradicting God's eternal truth. In the case of salvation, she would be considering virginity a work necessary for God to save her. "For by grace are ye saved through faith; and that not of yourselves: it is the gift of God" (Eph. 2:8).

If as a believer a woman or girl doubts God's ever using her because of lost virginity, she must replace that Satan-implanted concept with Scripture assurance: "If we confess our sins, he is faithful and just to forgive us our sins, and to cleanse us from all unrighteousness" (1 John 1:9).

For someone in either state of uncertainty, I'd urge you to go back to Matthew's record of Jesus' genealogy and note that every woman in it was pure only by God's grace.

It is abundantly clear in the Bible that God intends men and women alike to maintain sexual purity prior to marriage and that there is a unique scarring in the individual who does not. At the same time, however, Christ's precious blood has the power to cleanse from any and all sin.

Now let's move on. There comes a tug at my heart as I focus on Mary's response to Gabriel. She was so quick and positive! She had the brief word of an angel; she immediately believed and complied. We have the very Word of God Himself in sixty-six blessed books—how readily do we respond?

The matter of relationships also comes into play in Mary's story. We noted the importance of her cousin Elisabeth at a critical point. Our interpersonal connections as Christian women can powerfully influence both in the negative and the positive sense. Godly wisdom will guide us into friendships that strengthen our character and convictions while guarding us against those who would deplete our spiritual resources and weaken our walk. We need to think, too, of the other side of the coin: each of us has opportunity to reach out to other women who, because of chronological or spiritual age, need faithful mentoring in biblical thought and life. Churches and ministries would be far healthier and more effective if we women would activate spiritually helpful friendships.

The Magnificat, which burst from Mary's heart in Elisabeth's home, is not only a beautiful expression of her exalted feeling; it also holds within it inspiration for us individually. That inspiration comes from the focus so evident throughout: magnification of and praise for God. Mary did not magnify herself in the outpouring; instead, all her thoughts lauded God's greatness. Oh, that my words—and my life—do likewise. I find tremendous encouragement to praise in the Psalms. The gratitude and rejoicing so eloquently set forth in them enrich my own feeble attempts at expression.

As we think back to the full-spectrum development Jesus experienced while growing up, we might realize that Scripture's concise statement really can be expanded to form a parenting pattern for Christians. The Bible says that throughout His youth Jesus increased—grew, expanded, matured, improved—in the areas named. Each child God entrusts to Christian parents should do the same. Let's just run briefly through the phrases describing Jesus' youthful increasing.

Jesus increased in wisdom. Although the reference is not primarily to that which is intellectual, the mental development of our children must be carefully guarded and guided because wisdom is anchored in the mind. IQ, grades, and degrees are not the basic issue, although we who know the Lord certainly are responsible to Him for excellence in mental training for ourselves and our children. Every child is given to the parents, not to the state. It's sad enough that American children hardly even learn basic practical knowledge in history, English, and math, thanks to the dumbing down of public education. But far worse happens spiritually. No wisdom is available to children of whatever age in public educational institutions because the Bible is excluded. In such settings wisdom can't even begin.

> For the Lord giveth wisdom: out of his mouth cometh knowledge and understanding. (Prov. 2:6)

God doesn't uncork our brain and pour in wisdom, knowledge, and understanding: He gives all of those through His Word, the Bible. That must be the primary textbook throughout a child's entire educational career. Because America has banned the Bible from her educational system, Generations X and Y have minds devoid of light. We Christian parents bear responsibility for molding our children's minds to think scripturally and to apply Scripture light to every aspect of daily life. In that way they will, like Jesus, increase in wisdom.

Jesus increased in stature. Godly parents will carefully oversee the physical well-being of each child. Good nutrition, abundant exercise, and sufficient sleep must be consistent, providing for healthy bodies. Children's health generally has fallen drastically in America, thanks to microwave "meals," TV and video game addiction, and child-dictated bedtimes.

Jesus increased in favor with God. Favor with God comes through obedience to Him. God's favor is portrayed in Psalm 1:1–3.

Blessed is the man that walketh not in the counsel of the ungodly, nor standeth in the way of sinners, nor sitteth in the seat of the scornful. But his delight is in the law of the Lord; and in his law doth he meditate day and night. And he shall be like a tree planted by the rivers of water, that bringeth forth his fruit in his season; his leaf also shall not wither; and whatsoever he doeth shall prosper.

The Ten Commandments demand obeying parents, and a promise is given for those who do so. Parents must teach obedience from a child's earliest days through all the years he or she is in the home Although discipline needs to be prayerfully, wisely, and consistently exerted upon each child, it must also be modeled by both parents through their personal self-discipline. "Do as I say, not as I do" creates bitterness and rebellion.

> MARY IS PORTRAYED AS A WOMAN WHO THOUGHT DEEPLY ALL ALONG THE PATHWAY OF HER LIFE.

Jesus increased in favor with God and man. Favor with man infers positive social behavior and relationships. No child enters the world with the concern for others that creates consideration, kindness, and good manners. Instead, inherently strong "I-focus" must be re-formed. God's Word constantly highlights honoring others and living compassionately. Nor should a child's respectful attitude and behavior be only toward those outside the family. Remember that when Mary found Jesus in the temple after searching Jerusalem for Him, she essentially reminded Him of filial duty. That is a point at which many modern Christian mothers fail: allowing the child(ren) to behave and speak disrespectfully. Such parental weakness enables a child to disobey Scripture and to stand in danger of God's punishment:

> The eye that mocketh at his father, and despiseth to obey his mother, the ravens of the valley shall pick it out, and the young eagles shall eat it. (Prov. 30:17)

Beyond a parent's earning the child's respect, home training should also focus upon positive social skills. Consideration and respect for other people is largely communicated through mannerliness. The cruder and ruder the world, the brighter shines the light of Christian etiquette.

Each of the above points noted in Jesus' growth, when prayerfully mined for their spiritual gold, will provide a mother and father with abundant signposts for rearing their children to be effective servant-soldiers for Jesus Christ.

Then there are Mary's heart contemplations. She doesn't come across at all as a chatterer—but she is certainly portrayed as a woman who thought deeply all along the pathway of her life. That should be true of each of us. The rush of life and the glut of its busyness make contemplative living exceedingly difficult. Who among us wouldn't do well to "disconnect" regularly from the never-ceasing, technology-enhanced demands: turn off the cell phone; cancel cable or satellite delivery systems and unplug the television; sign off the computer; give away the VCR; hide the iPod. The resulting quiet would offer marvelous opportunity for genuine contemplative thinking.

Even the two recorded instances in which Mary was not wise in motivation and words can draw our attention to any mother's easily made error, that is, attempting to block a child from what God desires for him or her. The unique mother-child bond can be misused. In our day such misuse is often seen in overprotection, not letting the child suffer the consequences of wrongdoing. Yet when a mother so buffers her offspring, she denies them vital learning and character growth. Even worse, of course, is the parent who discourages a child's moving forward to prepare for or engage in life ministry. Such a parent is elevating selfish emotional desires over God's best for her child.

The closing scene of Mary's life in Scripture certainly presents a heart lesson for us. What courage she had! It's doubtful that a woman of Mary's temperament ever would have seen a crucifixion. But she probably had heard the Roman atrocity described. Then came the day when her child was to die. She could have chosen to stay away, to save her own emotions, to protect herself from the atmosphere of hatred that had built to frenzied intensity. All those concerns were swept aside in the great flood of her maternal love. It was fitting for Mary to be there on the hill called Golgotha. She had experienced Jesus' arrival on earth without comprehending how it could be; and now she experienced His earthly end without understanding why it must be. Imagine the strength it took to watch all that was done to her beloved Son! Many hearts broke with sorrow that day, but none could have been so deeply shattered as Mary's.

The emotional kaleidoscope through which Mary tumbled in Jesus' arrest, trial, condemnation, death, resurrection, and ascension did not destroy or derail her. She went on in faith, identifying and fellowshiping with Jesus' followers. Her presence in the upper room when the Holy Spirit descended upon the gathered disciples demonstrates that she moved forward from the devastation of Golgotha to be actively involved in spreading the blessed gospel of her risen, ever-living Savior.

Surely as she had known unique wounding of heart in losing her earthly lamb, so too she must have known immeasurable thrill in proclaiming Him the blessed, heavenly Lamb of God.

Chapter 2
ANNA

The next-earliest woman to see and recognize Jesus was an aged widow. Anna appears in Luke 2:36–38:

> And there was one Anna, a prophetess, the daughter of Phanuel, of the tribe of Aser: she was of a great age, and had lived with an husband seven years from her virginity; and she was a widow of about fourscore and four years, which departed not from the temple, but served God with fastings and prayers night and day. And she coming in that instant gave thanks likewise unto the Lord, and spake of him to all that looked for redemption in Jerusalem.

An ordinary writer would have crafted sentence after sentence to present Anna and the thrilling incident in which she appears. The Bible uses few words, painting a concise but clear picture. Let's explore the dimensions of Anna indicated in the passage.

Of the four Gospel writers, God moved only Luke to record this particular woman's contact with Jesus. It's really not surprising that the three other writers dismissed an event occurring in Jesus' infancy. Luke's writing, however, reflects his interest in details of personal history. God wanted us to glimpse Anna's response to His Son.

Anna means "grace," and this dear woman's life demonstrated God's nearness and enabling. She was at the other end of life's spectrum from Mary: Anna was old—eighty-four years old. Yet Scripture subtly, deftly points back to her long-ago youth as being morally pure. She had "lived with an husband seven years from her virginity." What an interesting reference to her youthful sexual purity.

Do you suppose maintaining one's virginity was any easier or more popular in the first century than in the twenty-first? I don't. Rome ruled, and though the era produced impressive structures, widespread military conquests, and numerous technical advancements, Roman society itself was cancerous with sin. The character of those who govern influences those governed. Nor were the Jews themselves praiseworthy in terms of morality. Their greatest consistency, like ours, was in disobeying God's law. Jehovah repeatedly railed against Israel's adoption of pagan lifestyles. In light of those realities, then, a young woman faced considerable challenges in choosing and maintaining sexual purity. God moved Luke to note Anna's success in that important aspect of life. Why? Because by that indication we surmise that she had a heart right toward God prior to her life in the temple.

Despite her praiseworthy early life, sorrow and hardship swept in upon Anna: her husband died after they'd been married only seven years. As most married women would agree, it takes at least ten years for a man and his wife to adapt thoroughly to each other. Applying that rule of thumb to Anna can help us sympathize with what must have been her shock and devastation when widowed. Too, she apparently was childless.

Left a young widow, Anna neither sought another husband nor returned to her family for succor. Rather, she chose to dedicate herself to God's service.

~ She didn't become a gossip, hearing and passing on all the news rife in the circles of women.

~ She didn't allow bitterness over her loss to take root in her heart, drying her spirit and sharpening her tongue.

~ She didn't surround herself with frivolity or self-indulgence.

She went apart from the ordinary pursuits and pleasures of life, choosing to live within the temple. That choice reveals Anna to be a woman of God-focused heart and settled mind.

Temple living for Anna wasn't just a matter of quiet, monastic contemplation, an escape from the hubbub and pressures of secular life. Rather, she gave herself to constant spiritual labor. Stop a moment to reflect upon your own experience: ultimately, don't you find that the comings and goings, the doings and hearings, the efforts and pressures of daily life with family, co-workers, and friends demand less than the spiritual dimension of your existence? Body, mind, and heart more readily engage in outward focus and activity than in matters of the spirit. It's tough to spend time really concentrating on Bible study and prayer, isn't it? In fact, keeping oneself spiritually active, growing, and effective is the hardest thing any one of us has to do: our human structure and our world legislate against such concentration. Though the temple offered a spiritual atmosphere, the self Anna took there was entirely human. Therefore, her temple life indicates solid self-discipline.

The pain of bereavement had the potential to make Anna a temple-dweller who did nothing but salve her own wounds. Instead, she gave herself to a life of ministry. She was a "prophetess"—a forth-teller of God's truth. According to the practice and culture of that day, she no doubt had an important ministry to the women who came to the temple. She would have listened to their problems, encouraged them toward right decisions, and taught them eternal principles from the Scripture scrolls. As any ministry woman today will confirm, giving out in those ways is demanding: shared heartaches and problems mean weights of concern for the hearer, and godly counseling involves tremendous responsibility.

But the passage tells us more about Anna. Her dedication was total. Involvement as listener and advisor didn't fit into an 8:00–5:00 time frame, after which she could retire to her room and enjoy long hours of quiet and recouping. The passage indicates that she wasn't just a daytime servant of God; she served Him, rather, around the clock: "but served God . . . night and day."

Moreover, her service was the most rigorous type any of us can know: "with fastings and prayers."

Sublimating her own physical needs through fasting and denying self-focus in order to pray for others were constants for Anna. I suspect, too, that often her prayers included petitions for the Messiah's coming.

So there she was—in her chosen place, involved in her chosen vocation, focused upon her chosen object of affection—Jehovah Himself. Although in these many ways Anna seems an excellent candidate for seeing prophecy fulfilled, at the same time she was also highly unlikely for such privilege. She was a quiet-living old woman pretty well forgotten by the busy, bustling members of Jerusalem's society. If any of those secular folks gave thought to Anna at all, they probably considered her a bit odd and perhaps pitied her for all the "important" aspects of life she was missing. As for the religious community, it too would have thought little of

Anna. She was, after all, a woman—a negligible creature tending to relatively unimportant needs of other negligible creatures.

The Scripture description of Anna's highly dramatic experience is brief: "And she coming in that instant gave thanks likewise unto the Lord" (2:38a).

When was "that instant"? It was the moment of dedication for a baby. The infant Jesus had been circumcised in accordance with the law at eight days old, Mary had observed the prescribed forty days of purification following the birth, and now the parents had brought their baby boy to the temple. They were dedicating Him to the Lord with the offering poor people were to bring: a pair of turtledoves, or two young pigeons. Though this One newly come from the landscape of eternity was the creator God in human flesh, the law was not set aside for Him—rather, He would fulfill the law from beginning to end, in every aspect, and to a degree that no other human being ever had, will, or could.

And "that instant" involved another person: Simeon, just and devout, waiting faithfully for the Messiah's appearing. The Holy Spirit motivated Simeon to enter the temple just in time to witness the eternally strategic moment when the baby Jesus was to be dedicated. How many years, months, and days had he patiently waited, trusting the Spirit's promise that he would see the Messiah? How many days had he left the temple in empty disappointment? But now, at last, there was "that instant." The old man took the baby in his arms and burst out with wonderful words of recognition and praise:

> Lord, now lettest thou thy servant depart in peace, according
> to thy word: for mine eyes have seen thy salvation, which thou
> hast prepared before the face of all people; a light to lighten the
> Gentiles, and the glory of thy people Israel. (2:29–32)

Simeon's exclamation clearly shows that the Holy Spirit had not only led him into the temple for that promised moment but He had also shed the light of heavenly understanding into his mind. As a Jew, he greeted the Jewish baby as the long-anticipated Messiah of the Jews but also as the Savior of the Gentiles—haters and persecutors of the Jews. Simeon's comprehension of Messiah's universal provision of salvation predated others' by decades.

That was the moment Anna came into the same part of the temple. Imagine yourself with those four people and the baby; gooseflesh rises, doesn't it? See the old woman, perhaps bent with the years and stiff with age-hardened joints, move forward . . . pull the blanketing wrap from about the little head . . . look into the face of the eternal God—and know Him for Who He is.

By the time of His dedication other people around Mary and Joseph had seen little Jesus; they had seen only a baby—apparently like any other baby. Anna, however, instantly knew Him to be no ordinary child. Why? How? Because through all the preceding years she had dedicatedly looked into the face of Jehovah. She had used those lonely years to grow closer and closer to Him, to learn more and more of His heart and His mind. I don't believe Anna was shocked as she saw the baby face that day—but overwhelmingly delighted and completely fulfilled in seeing Jehovah in the flesh. And Scripture describes her response: "She . . . gave thanks likewise unto the Lord" (2:38*b*).

Her heart and lips joyfully seconded Simeon's ecstatic acknowledgement of deity come to dwell with and in humanity.

Before ever a word came from His mouth, long before He was grown to manhood to do miraculous works and speak marvelous words, Jesus profoundly influenced Anna. That influence is seen in the final phrase of the passage: "And spake of him to all them that looked for redemption in Jerusalem" (2:38*c*).

Anna's life prior to seeing the Christ child appears to have been primarily behind the scenes—quietness, fasting, and prayer. But, having seen—and recognized—the longed-for Messiah, she went public: she became a proclaimer of fulfilled prophecy "to all them that looked for redemption in Jerusalem" (2:38c).

That phrase refers to any of the city's Jewish population with whom she had contact! Groaning under the grinding heel of Roman oppression, Jews longed for Jehovah to fulfill His promise of rescue.

Anna didn't trumpet her experience. She had been highly honored by Jehovah. She had known a moment of unparalleled emotion. But because she was genuinely godly, she drew no attention to herself: she proclaimed Him—and Him only.

Have you ever wondered about the reception of Anna's proclamations? No doubt it varied tremendously. Some of her hearers would have dismissed her words out of hand, not giving them a second thought. Others would have looked at her askance, convinced that her years in the temple had loosed her mental moorings. Some few would have contemplated her claims briefly, then dismissed them with a sigh, thinking this just another of the many mistaken "identifyings" of Messiah. After all, they could look back upon a number of men who in earlier years gave evidence of unusual character or power and who drew a following of those who thought them the long-awaited One come from God. Yet some others would have mocked at the idea of a baby—particularly a peasant baby—being the king for whom they yearned. But surely a few—probably a very few—would have listened to Anna, taken her godly character and faithful life into account, and grasped, however feebly, at the truth.

Whatever and wherever the responses, Anna wasn't responsible for those—she was responsible only for her personal testimony. And she faithfully bore that testimony.

Meeting Him with Her

Although all of Anna's widowed years were spent tucked away in the temple, her life reaches across the centuries to challenge us.

We should be challenged to maintain sexual purity. Such living is increasingly attacked by the ungodly world. Women in the public eye not only vaunt their live-in relationships but brazenly publicize their out-of-wedlock pregnancies. The world at large has become a cesspool of sexual immorality. We are experiencing life's degradations "as in the days of Noah." And, sad to say, to a great degree Christians participate in the ways of the days. Teachers in Christian junior high schools tell me that sexual intercourse is considered "stylish" in seventh and eighth grade. Virginity has come to be considered unimportant, excessive, archaic, unrealistic. Where did that attitude originate? Certainly not with God! Throughout His Word sexual purity is demanded, while fornication and adultery are not only condemned but are also declared to be particularly destructive: "But whoso committeth adultery with a woman lacketh understanding: he that doeth it destroyeth his own soul. A wound and dishonour shall he get; and his reproach shall not be wiped away" (Prov. 6:32–33).

The case for sexual purity doesn't apply only to girls and young women. It is a Bible standard for each of us at whatever age. For those of us who are older, the crux of the matter may come down to our mind, rather than our body. Jesus presented a powerful reality about sexual purity to men in Matthew 5:27–28: "Ye have heard that it was said by them of old time, Thou shalt not commit adultery: but I say unto you, That whosoever looketh on a woman to lust after her hath committed adultery with her already in his heart."

The principle enunciated by the Lord that day is not exclusively for men. It applies to us women as well. What's more, the danger of violating it is extremely high in our day through the media and modern technology. You and I have twenty-four-hour sexual indulgences available. When we allow those sources to invade our thoughts and imaginations, we violate our God-demanded purity, and we commit that which is abominable in His sight.

No matter how pervasively available prurient materials may be, we choose to accept or refuse their entrance into eyes, ears, and mind. We're thus guilty before God, must repent, and redirect our thinking.

Protecting ourselves against mental sexual impurity means more than just mounting a guard against blatantly degrading materials. It also demands the discernment to recognize subtle presentations. I've recently become concerned about a genre that goes under the title of "Christian Romance." The seeming innocence is a smokescreen that obscures its impure effects. While the material presents a purportedly spiritual theme, the story line and characters lure the reader into unclean thoughts and mental pictures. "Dearly beloved, I beseech you as strangers and pilgrims, abstain from fleshly lusts, which war against the soul" (1 Pet. 2:11). Besides

Anna's sexual morality, we can also see in her a shining example of godly widowhood.

In terms of spiritual decisions, what's a woman to do when her husband dies? Each time my Bible-reading brings me to 1 Timothy 5, I pause over one section in particular. As part of his instruction to the young pastor, Timothy, Paul wrote:

> But the younger widows refuse: for when they have begun to wax wanton against Christ, they will marry; having damnation, because they have cast off their first faith. And withal they learn to be idle, wandering about from house to house; and not only idle, but tattlers also and busybodies, speaking things which they ought not. (1 Tim. 5:11–13)

Earlier verses make it clear that a local body of believers has responsibility to care for older godly women whose husbands have died and whose own family cannot support them. But the same does not apply to younger widows. Notice the apostle's warning tone: it indicates unflattering characteristics and behavior in younger widows. Paul's reference to those negatives must indicate his observation of and dealing with such problems. The Timothy passage can serve as a contrasting portrait to that of Anna, indicating what she had chosen against. The contrast becomes clear as we take it phrase by phrase.

"When they have begun to wax wanton against Christ" (5:11). Whatever the reason for her husband's death, a godly young Christian widow would initially take her sorrow and confusion to the Lord. Suddenly deprived of dependence upon her husband, his death would be the catalyst for a near-desperate turning to the Lord. Such extremities in life awaken us to heart needs that only God can meet. A reliant relationship with Him becomes essential and proves to be wonderfully effective. But because of universal fleshly weakness, a young widow may over time choose to look less strongly to the Lord and to look, instead, at her own changed state, at still-whole marriages around her, at whatever her widowhood means in terms of pressures and difficulties. By such a weakened focus and reliance, she "waxes wanton" against Christ. She begins to look elsewhere for sustenance and fulfillment. Anna didn't.

"They will marry, having damnation, because they have cast off their first faith" (5:11*b*–12). This indictment harks back to God's earliest dealings with His chosen people. In Deuteronomy 6 Moses conveys Jehovah's clear instructions to His people. In each call to faithfulness and obedience, God's heart desire is clear: "That it may be well with thee, and that ye may increase mightily" (6:3*a*).

Then comes the core demand: "And thou shalt love the Lord thy God with all thine heart, and with all thy soul, and with all thy might" (6:5).

An exclusive, tenacious love relationship is God's aim for each of us who claims to be His child. It's in that light the young widow who remarries is condemned: she has thereby betrayed her divine lover.

Having castigated the youthful widow's distracted heart, Paul goes on to describe the behavior springing from such a heart. "And withal they learn to be idle, wandering about from house to house" (1 Tim. 5:13*a*).

Any woman with weakening heart attachment to God gives room to other things—negative invaders. Isn't it interesting that the first fault named in a widow's cooled devotion to God is idleness. For years that seemed to me a rather strange and somewhat minor thing. But it's not at all. God created human beings to be doers. His very first man and woman, Adam and Eve, didn't laze in the Garden of Eden. They exercised dominion over "every living thing that moveth upon the earth" (Gen. 1:28). But God also added to that assignment: "And the Lord God took the man, and put him into the garden of Eden to dress it and to keep it" (2:15).

So even in a perfect setting, human beings were to be occupied in practical and useful ways. When sin entered, making the earth and all upon it dying things, human occupation efforts intensified exponentially.

The Bible repeatedly commends diligence and condemns slothfulness in life's practical matters. "Slothfulness casteth into a deep sleep; and an idle soul shall suffer hunger" (Prov. 19:15).

Even in spiritual matters we're told to be diligent. "Keep thy heart with all diligence; for out of it are the issues of life" (Prov. 4:23).

In Old Testament times believers needed to work actively to maintain their relationship with Jehovah. The same is true in our New Testament era: the Bible's instructions for a God-pleasing life demand tremendous effort. "Therefore we ought to give the more earnest heed to the things which we have heard, lest at any time we should let them slip" (Heb. 2:1).

Physical and spiritual indolence are closely connected. That's why Paul warned against young widows growing idle. He went on to point out specific negative results of idleness: wandering from house to house and becoming busybodies.

People of either gender, of whatever active age, who have too much time on their hands, get into trouble themselves and create trouble with and for others.

We can observe the sad effects of idleness everywhere around us—particularly among teenagers. As a general rule, young people are not given responsibility or taught to work; instead, they occupy their out-of-school hours with TV, movies, electronic games, the Internet . . . flaccid in body and brain, these pathetic youngsters fall or drift into ever-more-degraded current lifestyles.

Interestingly, Generation Y is the term applied to American young people—and idleness is one of the indicators of the generations representing the end of civilization's alphabet.

ANY OF US WOMEN CAN EASILY BE LURED BY NUMEROUS, EVER-PRESENT OPPORTUNITIES FOR IDLENESS.

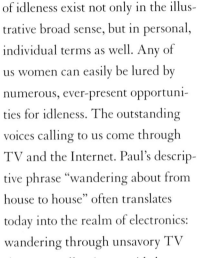

The characteristics and dangers of idleness exist not only in the illustrative broad sense, but in personal, individual terms as well. Any of us women can easily be lured by numerous, ever-present opportunities for idleness. The outstanding voices calling to us come through TV and the Internet. Paul's descriptive phrase "wandering about from house to house" often translates today into the realm of electronics: wandering through unsavory TV dramas, soap operas, and talk shows as well as into vapid chat rooms and mind-defiling blogs.

Still another fallout from idleness is misuse of the mouth. Though you and I may smile indulgently over or joke about the "little" sin of gossip, God doesn't. He makes that clear in moving Paul to speak out against young widows who are "not only idle, but tattlers also, and busybodies, speaking things which they ought not" (1 Tim. 5:13*b*).

When a woman's mind and body are not engaged in worthwhile activity, her curiosity reaches out into the "interesting" lives of others; she monitors, evaluates, and publicizes things that are none of her business. Long before Paul wrote to Timothy, Solomon's proverbs had similarly skewered gossip, as for example in Proverbs 26:20, 22: "Where there is no talebearer, the strife ceaseth. . . . The words of a talebearer are as wounds, and they go down into the innermost parts of the belly."

God's warning in 1 Timothy 5 does not serve as a flat-footed prohibition against a widow's remarriage. It certainly should, however, cause a widow of whatever age to consider the matter at length and in depth. A further urging in this regard is found in 1 Corinthians 7:39–40:

> The wife is bound by the law as long as her husband liveth; but if her husband be dead, she is at liberty to be married to whom she will; only in the Lord. But she is happier if she so abide, after my judgment: and I think also that I have the Spirit of God.

Paul also makes remarriage distinctions on the basis of age: "I will therefore that the younger women marry, bear children, guide the house, give none occasion to the adversary to speak reproachfully" (1 Tim. 5:14). The great apostle recognized that a woman's chronological youth may also indicate her spiritual immaturity with its vulnerability to the dangers mentioned earlier.

In her young widowhood Anna chose not to go the easy way. Her decision made an enormous impact within her and around her through all the years to follow! While working on this chapter, I had an interesting conversation with a woman who is a modern Anna. Cindy and her husband met while studying here at Bob Jones University and were married shortly after graduation. He went on to complete an advanced degree, and the young couple went out to plant a church. However, after only ten months in his pastorate aggressive cancer snuffed out his earthly life. Cindy made choices paralleling Anna's. She chose active service for Christ and returned to her alma mater. For sixteen years she has been here devoting her life to young college women—first as a residence supervisor and now as a teacher. In speaking with me about her life investment in ministry as a widow, she glowingly tells of the contentment and fulfillment with which the Lord has rewarded her choice of living singly for Him.

Finally—and in fact core to Anna—is her upward-focused heart, the habit of which prepared her to recognize the infant Jesus as the promised Messiah. The temple dedication took place in a moment; she had been developing her heart's clear-sightedness over the long years that lay behind. You and I need to emulate Anna's faithful daily focus upward to the face of God. The driving force behind our focus should be that which was expressed so powerfully by the apostle Paul: "That I may know him, and the power of his resurrection, and the fellowship of his sufferings, being made conformable unto his death" (Phil. 3:10).

The temple is gone, the infant Jesus grew to mature manhood and, in measureless love, paid the price for our salvation. But we need to recognize Him present in each circumstance of our life. When we are able to see Him there, we—like dear Anna—are able to accept . . . to endure . . . to rejoice . . . and to give testimony of and for Him.

> For now we see through a glass, darkly; but then face to face: now I know in part; but then shall I know even as also I am known. (1 Cor. 13:12)

Chapter 3

THE SAMARITAN WOMAN

Years of silence lay between Anna's recognizing the infant Jesus and His first recorded meeting as an adult with a woman. Too, a great gap of difference can be seen between the meeting places: the first was the temple in Jerusalem, the next a city well-side in Sychar. And how different the women: Anna the devout widow versus the Samaritan, a woman of multiple relationships both legal and illegal. Come now to the spot where Jesus met the latter.

> He left Judea, and departed again into Galilee. And he must needs go through Samaria. Then cometh he to a city of Samaria, which is called Sychar, near to the parcel of ground that Jacob gave to his son Joseph. Now Jacob's well was there. (John 4:3–6a)

Thus John sets the scene. Today the place name *Samaria* means "little." But in Jesus' day the word, the region, and its people held great meaning—and all of it negative. Samaria and Samaritans were held in contempt by Jews of surrounding areas. Why? Because the Assyrian captivity had populated Samaria with a mixed race—part Jewish, part Gentile. Due to their mixed blood Samaritans were unable to trace their genealogical roots—and thus drew intense racial prejudice. Lineage-proud Jews considered Samaria such a hateful place they even disliked traveling through it. The people of the land were considered little better than dogs. Some Pharisees went so far as to pray that no Samaritan would have a part in the resurrection.

So Jesus was in an unfriendly, foreign, and despised land. "Jesus therefore, being wearied with his journey, sat thus on the well: and it was about the sixth hour" (4:6b). It was high noon. In that Middle Eastern land midday is typically hot. And hunger no doubt gnawed at Him: "For his disciples were gone away unto the city to buy meat" (4:8).

But He wasn't allowed to enjoy either privacy or rest: "There cometh a woman of Samaria to draw water" (4:7a). The woman approaching the well was one of the most wholly foreign Jesus is recorded as having met. She certainly didn't fit an ideal pattern of femininity. Women of the time—even female servants—didn't do their water-collecting in the middle of the day. Instead, they used the cooler hours of early morning or evening, and their daily well-side gatherings took on the nature of social events. This woman's solitary appearance at noon signaled that she was one of Sychar's fringe citizens. Yet Jesus took no evasive action; He took the initiative and spoke to her: "Jesus saith unto her, Give me to drink" (4:7b).

His recognition of her was highly unusual, as men rarely spoke to any woman in public. Certainly a decent man did not address a woman whose tarnished reputation was evident. No wonder she was surprised by His speaking to her.

However, before proceeding with the story, let's move in imagination back along the path that brought the Samaritan woman to Jacob's well that day. Picture her likely home setting. It's impossible to consider the multiple marriages meaning any kind of improvement from one to the next. Rather, they would have been a downward spiral, with each succeeding husband worse in every way than the last. And now she cohabited with a man she'd not even bothered to marry. All feminine pride and hope must have been gone. Her existence in such a house and such a relationship had to be dismal. And the necessary daily trip to the well would have offered little if any lightening of her gloom because she went as a marked woman, avoided by decent citizens. What a lonely figure! I can hear in her words a snappishness born of dreariness, self-disgust, and resentment of others. Very likely, too, her gut reaction would have been that any Jewish stranger would address her only as a preliminary to sexual solicitation.

> Then saith the woman of Samaria unto him, How is it that
> thou, being a Jew, askest drink of me, which am a woman of
> Samaria? for the Jews have no dealings with the Samaritans.
> (4:9)

Jesus immediately halted and redirected her thoughts: "If thou knewest the gift of God, and who it is that saith to thee, Give me to drink; thou wouldest have asked of him, and he would have given thee living water" (4:10*b*).

That single sentence is packed with spiritual meaning. The woman spoke of the enormous chasm of religious form separating Jews and Samaritans. Jesus pulled her attention away from conflicting formal rites to a personal relationship that gifts the human participant with life-giving water. And where she spoke of Jewish and Samaritan people groups, He focused on Himself and her in an individualized personal transaction.

What a jolt! From dust and heat, discouragement and disgust to the thought of a gracious gift from God! And rising up through

her surface hardness came a sensitive response. Notice her change
of tone: "Sir, thou hast nothing to draw with, and the well is deep:
from whence then hast thou that living water?" (4:11*b*).

"Sir"—a respectful form of address greatly unlike her earlier
rude, challenging words. Obviously, she was puzzled: the Jew
talked of giving water, but He was without any means of drawing
it! This woman with the battered, shameful life was no dullard:
listen to the aroused interest and the careful hearing indicated
in her words, "From whence then hast thou that living water?"
She seems somehow to have perceived the spiritual connotation
of *water*—particularly since the term He used and she repeated
was "living water." What a tantalizing term to a woman whose
existence was so stiflingly dust-laden.

But then came an emotional step back, as if seeking escape
from the moment of vulnerability. After all, she would have
reminded herself, any Jew's dealing with a Samaritan could only
be mockery and down-putting. So she returned to her earlier spirit
of challenge. "Art thou greater than our father Jacob, which gave
us the well, and drank thereof himself, and his children, and his
cattle?" (4:12).

Although living on the fringes of Sychar's society, she was
made of Samaria's fabric, and she resorted to that fabric as if
drawing it about her for protection from this strange man and his
strange conversation.

Jesus was not distracted by her snippy words but continued to
employ the water analogy so apt in the setting in which they con-
versed. "Whosoever drinketh of this water shall thirst again: but
whosoever drinketh of the water that I shall give him shall never
thirst; but the water that I shall give him shall be in him a well of
water springing up into everlasting life" (4:13*b*–14). The drought
in the woman's soul made her yearn for the kind of refreshing

pictured in the stranger's words. "The woman saith unto him Sir, give me this water, that I thirst not, neither come hither to draw" (4:15).

Can't you hear her thirst of soul and her longing for the end of those daily trips to the well with its gauntlet of pointing fingers, whispered gossip, and pulled-aside shoulders by fellow citizens of Sychar? How greatly this woman's soft heart contrasted with her hard exterior! Jesus spoke only a few words: yet she reached out with open hands toward what He offered.

Receiving the marvelous quenching, however, was to be more than a simple transaction. She must be made to realize the extent of her need. The Lord focused her thinking upon the most thoroughly parched part of her life. "Jesus saith unto her, Go, call thy husband, and come hither" (4:16).

I don't know how the woman could have heard those words without groaning inwardly. After all, it was her blatant immorality that forced her to make such miserable noontime trips to the well. Call her husband? If only such simplicity were possible! The stranger's request probed to the core of what she was and how she lived. Conviction made her offer Him a partial truth. "The woman answered and said, I have no husband" (4:17a).

Did she try to intone maidenly innocence in those four words? Was the brief statement a verbal shrug attempting to dismiss the subject? Or was the brevity due to a choking conviction? How she must have hoped the matter would be left there, that the conversation would move on to disclose the secret for receiving the marvelous water offered to her. But there was no moving on, no release from the sudden tension in their exchange.

"Jesus said unto her, Thou hast well said, I have no husband: for thou hast had five husbands; and he whom thou now hast is not thy husband: in that saidst thou truly" (4:17b–18). Jesus took her four words and trapped her in them. Consider the fascinating process: "Thou hast well said"—He gently opened the trap-door. "I have no husband"—there's the innocuous bait: her own statement. "For thou hast had five husbands; and he whom thou now hast is not thy husband"—the bait was exposed as rotten and dangerous. "In that saidst thou truly"—the door of the trap bangs shut on the hinges of her own expression.

As in the case of a captured animal, the Samaritan woman didn't immediately freeze in surrender. Since Jesus had so thoroughly exposed her sinfulness, she had to acknowledge Him to be more than an ordinary person: "Sir, I perceive that thou art a prophet" (4:19*b*).

The words are almost laughable as we read them. And yet I believe the context shows her response to be a step toward belief. Her opinion had moved far from the original concept of Him as a Jew who was either baiting her or considering solicitation. She had come to see Him as a person of spiritual character and ability. But she wanted His spiritual perception to focus somewhere other than upon her sin. So she tried throwing a red herring. Surely long-standing disagreement about the proper place to worship Jehovah would turn the conversation away from His convicting focus on her. "Our fathers worshipped in this mountain; and ye say, that in Jerusalem is the place where men ought to worship" (4:20).

Jesus of course was not distracted. I think His presentation here is highly interesting. As in the earlier instances, He took her own expressed thought and built upon it. The more I soak in the conversational exchange, the more my mind moves back to one of Isaiah's presentations of God's seeking heart: "Come now, and let us reason together, saith the Lord: though your sins be as scarlet, they shall be as white as snow; though they be red like crimson, they shall be as wool" (Isa. 1:18).

Hear that "reasoning together." Jesus first decimated the woman's attempt to get His focus onto the long-standing controversy between Jews and Samaritans. Next He pointed out the dilution into meaninglessness of Samaritan belief: "Ye worship ye know not what" (4:22a). He went on to declare Israel's correct focus in worship: "We know what we worship" (4:22b).

I imagine a change then in Jesus' vocal tone as He—a Jew and the preeminent Jew—spoke the next phrase: "For salvation is of the Jews" (4:22c).

Then came a major transition indicated by the word *but*— "But the hour cometh" (4:23a).

Having begun earlier by indicating an approaching spiritual change, He here repeated the thought "the hour cometh," then declared the noted change to be immediate: "And now is" (4:23b).

Note how closely the topics of salvation's Jewish source and changed worship appear in the presentation. Imagining myself standing with the Samaritan woman, I sense in her a sharpening of attention . . . perhaps a quickening of her heartbeat as Jesus quietly, pointedly continued:

> True worshippers shall worship the Father in spirit and in truth: for the Father seeketh such to worship him. God is a Spirit: and they that worship him must worship him in spirit and in truth. (4:23–24)

"The Father seeketh"—how warmly those words must have been spoken. How enticing must have been the glimpse of a borderless, conflict-free, personal approach to and adoration of God.

I wonder if perhaps her doubly despised state as a Samaritan and as an immoral woman made her particularly receptive to the concept of God seeking beyond ordinary, surface identities to the inner reality of spirit and truth. "The woman saith unto him,

I know that Messias cometh, which is called Christ: when he is come, he will tell us all things" (4:25).

She was taught in religious matters, and in the stranger's conversation she caught sight of Scripture's promised Messiah. I hear her words as low and hesitant, exposing her heart's tentative reach toward His identity as that prophesied One. How indescribably wonderful the truth revealed to her yearning heart! Jesus presented Himself to this shunned, wretched woman in simple, direct words: "I that speak unto thee am he" (4:26b).

Those seven brief words present the Father's saving pronouncement as recorded in Isaiah 43:25—"I, even I, am he that blotteth out thy transgressions for mine own sake, and will not remember thy sins."

And those seven words, the first direct identification of Himself as Messiah, were spoken to a woman—a woman to whom few people would even speak.

The conversation was interrupted by the disciples' return from the city with food. But the momentary exchange between the Man of Nazareth and the woman of Samaria had been long enough to accomplish its eternal purpose.

The disciples not only failed to understand the aura of quiet unity surrounding the woman and Jesus but also were appalled that there was any association at all. "And upon this came his disciples, and marvelled that he talked with the woman: yet no man said, What seekest thou? or, Why talkest thou with her?" (4:27).

The unspoken questions indicate that Jesus' followers looked in silent, disapproving puzzlement among themselves and at the two whose conversation they had interrupted.

The Samaritan woman had no chance for further time with the Nazarene. But she had recognized and received Him as the living Truth, and she wanted others to do likewise. "The woman then left her waterpot, and went her way into the city, and saith to the men, Come, see a man, which told me all things that ever I did: is not this the Christ?" (4:28–29).

I love the fact of the forgotten waterpot. Her heart's vessel was full to overflowing, and the vessel of clay had lost its significance. She went to the well a pariah; she went from it a proclaimer.

There is common sense evident in the fact that she told the wondrous news of Christ to the men of Sychar rather than to the women. Women would have been slow to drop their long-held hostility. The men, however, heard her and responded without the binding of feminine negative emotions.

So from the shadows of Sychar came one who drew many to the Light. Through one who left her waterpot beside the well came the free-flowing, cleansing water of the gospel. "And many of the Samaritans of that city believed on him for the saying of the woman, which testified, He told me all that ever I did. So when the Samaritans were come unto him, they besought him that he would tarry with them: and he abode there two days" (4:39–40).

Because of her testimony's effectiveness Jesus made an un-scheduled stay in an unlikely place, giving many the opportunity to meet Him as Savior.

Still, there were those who, though they had become believers, could not entirely lay aside antipathies of the past: "And many more believed because of his own word: and said unto the woman, Now we believe, not because of thy saying: for we have heard him ourselves, and know that this is indeed the Christ, the Saviour of the world" (4:41–42).

I doubt that the disavowals bothered this precious woman in the least! Public opinion would seem an insignificant, muddy puddle since she had drunk deep of the living water.

Meeting Him with Her

Water is essential to physical and spiritual life. Speaking of the latter, Jesus said in John 7:37, "If any man thirst, let him come unto me, and drink."

He and He alone offers living water, sufficient for spiritual life both temporal and eternal. What a gracious, unmerited invitation He extends! But note that it's an invitation only. God doesn't force our turning to Him for salvation or spiritual sustenance. He allows us free choice.

Following our acceptance of Christ, each of us daily draws from some water source for our soul. Like the woman of Sychar, Jesus would confront us regarding our choices. Surely He would ask us, "What water source do you choose? How do you draw from the source?"

We who are born-again Christians should daily seek God's living water—found in the deep well of His Word—to sustain and refresh us. Yet so often we turn elsewhere:

~ past personal experience

~ a radio or TV purveyor of opinions/advice

~ self-help books or magazine articles

~ devotional writings

~ advice from family or friends

~ the daily horoscope

When we go to any other source, we seriously err. Results are harmful and far-reaching. God chides His children for turning anywhere but to Him. Listen to what He says about our seeking other water sources: "For my people have committed two evils; they have forsaken me the fountain of living waters, and hewed them out cisterns, broken cisterns, that can hold no water" (Jer. 2:13).

Jeremiah provides measureless meaning from which we can benefit if we take the time and exercise the determination to do so. Let's explore some of its contents together.

What is a cistern, anyway? My dictionary has the following definition: "A receptacle for holding water or other liquid, especially a tank for catching and storing rainwater." A cistern is a human means of catching and keeping water—a product of man, not of God.

So think, first of all, of an unbroken cistern—which, obviously, represents its prime condition. Because it is a means of collection, it yields only what comes into it. Such a source, then, presents multiple opportunities for contamination of the collected water: pollution from the air through which rain falls, debris from nearby objects or sullying entities from incoming channels. Thus, from its very origin a cistern infers fouling. And its dangerous contents worsen as water stands in it: microorganisms multiply; scum accumulates on the water's surface; insects and small animals fall into it to die and rot. Those threaten a drinker even in a whole, unbroken cistern.

God's heart cry in Jeremiah goes further: He rebukes His people's use of broken cisterns. What a picture, and what conviction, sorrow, and repentance it should speak to our heart. Resorting to cisterns seems to be a tendency of our basic human structure, no matter how long we've known the Lord. Man-made sources of survival ultimately disintegrate, depleting even the polluted contents. So in order to draw from the container we are forced lower, seeking its muddy, corrupted depths.

In practical terms, how does a cistern's failing sustenance play out? The pathetic scenario is not at all rare. At first the drinker may seem as healthy as anyone: the corrupted intake affects only internal, unobservable aspects of her structure. All seems well to her and to those around her. As she repeatedly draws and drinks from the cistern, however, changes take place in her personal operating system. Unseen, her spiritual immune system weakens.

A WOMAN WHO HAS GENUINELY COME TO SALVATION RECOGNIZES AND LOVES THE PURE, FRESH FLOW OF TRUTH AS IT POURS FORTH.

Doubt breaches her defenses: questions against and irritations with Bible doctrine work their way into her mind. These start as microscopic germs, yet their mental and spiritual effects can be devastating. Who has not heard of the years-faithful wife who "suddenly" exits her marriage in favor of someone she has met online? Or the daughter of a ministry home who "suddenly" announces that she is a lesbian and at once becomes evangelistic for her brand of degradation. Or . . . Wretched results like these may seem beyond personal possibility. But they—and countless other horrific ends—can result when cistern-bred impurities weaken a woman's spiritual immunity, leaving her vulnerable.

The progression from immunity's first weakening to sin's full-blown, life-destroying disease may be slow, and it can be carefully disguised by pretended well-being in activities and words. Decline is present, however: spiritual health is deteriorating. A woman who has genuinely come to salvation through the blood of Jesus

Christ begins her spiritual walk in excitement and energy, delighting in the fountain of living water, the Bible. She recognizes and loves the pure, fresh flow of Truth as it pours forth. She faithfully seeks God's precepts and walks aware of her weaknesses, fortifying herself through study of and obedience to Scripture. She certainly doesn't ever plan to seek another source, nor can she imagine doing so. However, time and life's busyness can work in combination with fallen human nature to allow the Bible's input to be less and less essential. After all, other sources are more readily available and easier to understand, nor do they invoke disapproval, ridicule, and challenge like the Bible does. Alternative sources also often present opportunities for comradeship, relaxation, and egocentric fulfillment. The alternative source becomes established as a mainstay and its use grows ever more natural. Ah yes—natural. That's the problem. Cisterns hold supply for our natural self, whereas God's fountain of living water is of the Spirit and for our spiritual being. As we're reminded repeatedly throughout God's Word, our old nature and our new nature are in lifelong conflict. The old nature all too often proves stronger—particularly when we resort to sources of supply that are distanced from the fountain of living water.

Now to the second question that might be voiced by the Lord: How do we draw from the cistern or the well? The woman of Sychar came physically well-equipped for drawing from the town's water source: she brought a bucket. She also brought a bucket-sized heart, and the latter was filled, the former abandoned. Spiritually speaking, you and I tend to do the opposite. We bring a bucket or two to cisterns—that is, by spending hours studying some interesting psychological finding, enlightening aspect of temperament, or ten-step course that promises happily-ever-after relationships. Sometimes we even flop beside the cistern and press our face close to its contents.

And what of our spirit toward the fountain? Even when we discipline ourselves to access the Word each day, aren't we often satisfied to carry only a spoon rather than a bucket? We take just a sip—then we're off and running. Would we ever be found spiritually flopped on our belly, refreshing our whole face as we drink deeply of the forever-fresh water?

Finally in terms of the well at Sychar, what of the woman's leaving it? She went away not just temporarily refreshed but eternally redeemed. Nor did she hug that newness to herself: she proclaimed Jesus as the Messiah. She spoke of Him so persistently, so convincingly, that others came to see and hear the man at the well. She spoke so magnetically of the One she'd met that He spent two days showing Himself to be the blessed promised One, bringing many to belief. The woman of Sychar abandoned her empty water pot but took a heart filled with the Water of Life and shared its fresh, transforming purity.

How do you and I leave the well of living water? Are we so sparingly refreshed that we've no overflow to share? Or are we perhaps so sated with our own intake as to be immobile and silent?

As I contemplate Jesus' meeting the woman at Sychar's well, I think of the words of a song that can encourage us to partake of the Water of Life—and to let it flow through us to others. They're appropriate as part of what we can take away with us from the recorded well-side incident in Samaria.

CHANNELS ONLY

How I praise Thee, precious Saviour,
That Thy love laid hold of me;
Thou hast saved and cleansed and filled me
That I might Thy channel be.

Emptied that Thou shouldest fill me,
A clean vessel in Thy hand;
With no pow'r but as Thou givest
Graciously with each command.

Jesus, fill now with Thy Spirit
Hearts that full surrender know;
That the streams of living water
From our inner man may flow.

Channels only, blessed Master,
But with all Thy wondrous pow'r
Flowing thro' us, Thou canst use us
Ev'ry day and ev'ry hour.

Chapter 4
PETER'S MOTHER-IN-LAW

In the years between His birth and the beginning of His public ministry at the age of thirty, Jesus doubtless met numbers of men and women as He pursued the quiet life of a carpenter's apprentice. But those incidents, like most of His youth and young manhood, are left unrevealed. We have only simple, broad references—"And the child grew, and waxed strong in spirit, filled with wisdom: and the grace of God was upon him" (Luke 2:40).

Thirty was the God-determined age for beginning priestly ministry, so Jesus confirmed even this relatively small facet of the law. One of the women whom He met early in His ministry was Peter's wife's mother. She appears in three of the Gospels:

> And when Jesus was come into Peter's house, he saw his wife's mother laid, and sick of a fever. And he touched her hand, and the fever left her; and she arose, and ministered unto them. (Matt. 8:14–15)

> And forthwith, when they were come out of the synagogue, they entered into the house of Simon and Andrew, with James and John. But Simon's wife's mother lay sick of a fever, and

anon they tell him of her. And he came and took her by the hand, and lifted her up; and immediately the fever left her, and she ministered unto them. (Mark 1:29–31)

And he arose out of the synagogue, and entered into Simon's house. And Simon's wife's mother was taken with a great fever; and they besought him for her. And he stood over her, and re-buked the fever; and it left her: and immediately she arose and ministered unto them. (Luke 4:38–39)

Peter's mother-in-law—that is her only identification—and the setting—Peter's house in Capernaum—really holds all we're told of her existence. Yet God chose to highlight that momentary crossing of paths between Jesus and a woman. That highlighting signals significance. So let's consider her as she is presented and imagine some of the possibilities and probabilities of the situation, characters, and relationships involved.

Jesus and some of the disciples had come from the synagogue to Peter's house, where this woman and her condition came to His attention.

Why was Peter's mother-in-law there in his home? Was she visiting? If so, she likely would have been enjoying the time—until she fell ill—except that her visit demanded her daughter's extra time and attention.

Or was she a resident in the house? There is no father-in-law mentioned. Was he with her but not an important part of the story? Had he perhaps abandoned her? Or had he died? If her husband was totally out of the picture, this woman may have been resident by necessity because she was unable to support herself. Being taken into the home of a daughter and son-in-law was a common practice of the day when a parent was left widowed. If that were the case, and she as a widow lived in Peter's home, the situation might have had some uneasy aspects. Anyone who has enjoyed independence or husbandly support finds it difficult to give up that life and become dependent upon a child. Too, such dependence creates strictures upon the privacy and independence of the host home. No matter how kind the younger couple may have been in their treatment of and attitude toward her, a woman so placed must have experienced awkward moments, knowing that to some extent her presence was intrusive and burdensome.

A live-in situation would imply several things: She was a woman with needs of various kinds. If indeed she was a widow, there certainly would have been emotional matters involved as she bore the various burdens of loss. Judging by the fact that she had a married daughter, she must have been at least middle-aged with age-related needs. The middle years of life often prove to be a difficult time. A woman may feel that her reason for existence and her individual importance lie in the past, while the future looks uncertain. Likely, too, this woman would have felt it necessary to offset her enforced residency: an abiding sense of obligation would make her exert constant effort to "pay for her keep." It could even be that she had worked herself into the illness in which she comes to our attention.

Now think what meaning might possibly lie in the simple words identifying her as Peter's mother-in-law. Peter—that one of Jesus' disciples who from the outset was so quick in his reactions, so unadvisedly hasty in his words, that we in generations since have come to think of him as being redheaded with the fiery temperament such coloring implies. Imagine living with such a temperament. If Peter had been her birth son, that would be one thing, but he was her son-in-law, and the step-away relationship perhaps made his idiosyncrasies particularly irritating. Or rather than irritation, Peter's personality might have caused heart-felt sympathy for her daughter's difficult marriage. The in-law relationship might in itself foster a certain lack of mutual appreciation and understanding between her and Peter.

So there she was—for whatever reason—an "adjunct" in Peter's home. But Jesus did not treat her in any way as less important than any other household member or than one of His own disciples.

Beyond the difficulties possibly accruing from her being an outsider on the inside, there is a further complication to her situation: she was ill—so ill with fever that she was bedfast. If she was visiting, illness surely would have created disappointment and embarrassment for her. On the other hand, if she was resident in the home, she knew that being bedfast increased the burdensome aspect of her presence. In the latter case she may have felt emotionally battered because she was experiencing blow upon blow.

The Bible relates nothing of Jesus' own condition at the moment, but from the mention of His coming from the synagogue, evidently He had been preaching and teaching there. Those verbal activities may be thought minimal in terms of physical demands. But that's not so. Modern studies have determined that a good speaker uses as much energy in one hour as a ditch digger. We know, of course, that Jesus was the greatest speaker Who ever lived; books have been written detailing the technical excellence of His verbal presentations. So in His human structure He no doubt experienced post-speaking tiredness. But as He entered Peter's house that day, any anticipation for His physical rest gave way to her physical need.

The fever-racked woman must have been in a room apart from where He was meeting with His disciples because the disciples told Jesus about the woman's illness. He could have disregarded her as "out of sight, out of mind." He could have dismissed the disciples' words because of His own weariness. He might have thought the need—a fever—so minor it was unworthy of His attention. After all, earlier He had been engaged in major, dramatic healings. He did none of those dismissive things; instead He responded immediately to her plight. He went to her bedside.

Mother-in-law as a term may indicate this woman's lack of household focus, but she claimed full personal attention of God's Son. Jesus went to her bedside and took her by the hand. How warm and gentle that touch must have felt to her! At the same time how wonderful the instant cooling as the fever released its hold upon her body.

Notice that Luke's narrative tells us Jesus "rebuked the fever." I wonder why? The Bible makes clear that difficulties can be God's tools for bringing unbelievers to Him and for strengthening His children. It also tells us that everything in a believer's life is either sent or allowed by our heavenly Father. In light of those facts, did Jesus' rebuke

~ end the fever because it had sufficiently softened the woman's heart to hear and heed His message of eternal Truth?

~ end it in the sense of terminating Satan's troubling efforts?

~ end it with the inherent intention of making the woman know that she had made herself sick psychosomatically?

Take into account, next, the completeness of healing accomplished that day. Think back to a time when you had a fever making you bedfast. Its effects weren't limited to your downtime only, were they? Rather, there were lingering results—particularly, weakness from which it took some time to recover. Not so for Peter's mother-in-law. The fever ended, and simultaneously her strength returned.

In studying these short passages relating the incident with Peter's mother-in-law, I've wondered what this woman's attitude toward Jesus had been prior to their meeting at her bedside. What

if all she knew of Him had come through Peter? That might have
been off-putting! To hear her flamboyant, emotionally volatile son-
by-marriage tell of the Nazarene might have awakened negative
reactions. She could have had thoughts like the following:

~ Would a genuinely wise teacher have anything to do with
brash, testy Peter?

~ These things Peter claims for the Nazarene are typical of his
on-again-off-again temperament! Tomorrow all these great
enthusiasms will probably have waned.

~ What kind of a man would induce Peter to give up fishing—
my daughter's support—to traipse all over the countryside
with Him?

~ It's hard enough having people think us odd because of
Peter's personality. The more we're connected with this
Nazarene Jesus and His unusual teachings, the stranger
they'll think we are.

Whatever opinions or attitudes the woman held prior to Jesus'
visit, His direct effect upon her was evident. She was freed from
the fever that had plagued her. His touch brought instant physical
change. Was there spiritual change as well? I believe so—whether
in terms of salvation or dedication. The narrative ends in such
a way that we catch a glimpse of her character that is spiritually
positive: "She arose and served them" (4:39).

Think first what she didn't do—

~ elevate herself as an important person in the household
because of Jesus' dealing with her.

~ run out to get the attention and admiration of those who
heard of the miracle.

~ keep to her bed, taking advantage of the situation in order to
be served.

Instead, she demonstrated a spirit just the opposite of those: she got up from her sickbed, proverbially put on her apron, and went to work serving Jesus and others.

Meeting Him with Her

As we think in terms of personal application, a verse in the Psalms seems appropriate: "Oh how great is thy goodness, which thou hast laid up for them that fear thee; which thou hast wrought for them that trust in thee before the sons of men!" (Ps. 31:19).

Peter's mother-in-law was sort of an "et cetera" person. She was not in the mainstream of cultural, social, or relational importance. Chances are she'd have been considered unimpressive and unimportant; perhaps she was the object of pity by women near her own age who enjoyed happier circumstances. She certainly would have been outshone by her flamboyant son-in-law. But we human beings are the ones who create categories of worth and assign individuals to whatever labeled slots we consider appropriate. The incident with Peter's wife's mother underlines the fact that Jesus Christ knows no second-class citizens. There is tremendous encouragement and blessing in that for each of us. We women, in particular, can rejoice—each in her quiet, unspotlighted place of life ministry. To be the focus of God's attention lends us immeasurable and eternal importance. The Bible assures us that His attention is always on us—not just in a single incident as was recorded of Peter's mother-in-law.

Soaking in this woman's story also reminds me that no need is too small for the Savior's concern and response. Compared to the dramatic cases of blindness, deafness, crippling, and demon-possession with which Jesus concerned Himself, this woman's fever seems almost laughable. But He didn't laugh. He fulfilled her unexpressed need. And He does so with you and me. The Lord has time and again met the private, really intimate yearnings of my heart, and doubtless you've experienced the same thing. One of the "fevers" to feel Jesus' cooling touch repeatedly for me comes from conflicting responsibilities that often mark my calendar. Each incident finds me dithered by trying to keep responsibility ducks on the same pond, tightly bound by impending

TO BE THE FOCUS OF GOD'S ATTENTION LENDS US IMMEASURABLE AND ETERNAL IMPORTANCE.

deadlines, discombobulated by drought-dry personal resources—and my heart lurches into fever mode. Then the dear Lord, in His never-failing tenderness and longsuffering, touches my distraction-heated heart and banishes the fever. The cooling of His peace sweeps in before I've even asked. A tiny need—met by His titanic supply.

A sort of adjunct conviction rises from the incident of Peter's mother-in-law as well. It has to do with her possible opinions about and reactions to the Savior because of Peter's unconscious temperament testimony. Just as in his case so long ago, you and I today sully or sanctify God to those around us. Our words, attitudes, and actions reveal our temperament and personality. Every genetic-plus-acquired persona has both positive and negative characteristics. Unfortunately we tend to express the latter more readily than the former. If that resulted only in a dented personal reputation, it would be bad enough. But for the born-again individual there's a further, far more important consideration: the reputation of the Lord Jesus. And yes, each life does contribute to or detract from that. When Peter's mother-in-law met Jesus Himself, His divine personhood, purity, and power were unmistakable. But when she only knew of—and judged—Him by Peter, His disciple, how very different He must have seemed. As you and I represent Jesus Christ day by day, how do we color His reputation?

The mother of Peter's wife experienced healing that day. She was freed from her fever. And Scripture shows her faithfully and wisely acting within her freed state. "For, brethren, ye have been called unto liberty; only use not liberty for an occasion to the flesh, but by love serve one another" (Gal. 5:13). The day in which we live more and more finds Christians misusing and abusing the blessed liberty Christ has given. They cater to fleshly desires and cultural dictates, dishonestly excusing themselves on the basis of "being free from the law."

The final thing that strikes me as I read of Peter's mother-in-law is her getting out of bed to serve Jesus and other people. As my husband and I listen to and try to encourage ministry folks, we constantly hear that their churches—solid, Bible-preaching churches—are filled with Christians who could suitably be termed "bedbugs." They're set upon living a life of spiritual relaxation; they see to it that despite abounding opportunities and exhortations, they remain cozily tucked in, demanding to be pampered. What's wrong with that picture? What's wrong with me when I yearn to do likewise? I imagine I hear the voice of Peter's mother-in-law echoing through the centuries: "If you've been healed, get up and serve!"

Chapter 5

THE WIDOW OF NAIN

O f the Gospel writers, only Luke records the incident of the widow of Nain. Surely his medical training and interests made restoration of life highly significant. Whatever the case humanly speaking, God determined that it should be part of the canon of Scripture. Therefore, there is gold to be mined if we labor to find and bring it to the surface.

> And it came to pass the day after, that he went into a city called Nain; and many of his disciples went with him, and much people. Now when he came nigh to the gate of the city, behold, there was a dead man carried out, the only son of his mother, and she was a widow: and much people of the city was with her. And when the Lord saw her, he had compassion on her, and said unto her, Weep not. And he came and touched the bier: and they that bare him stood still. And he said, Young man, I say unto thee, Arise. And he that was dead sat up, and began to speak. And he delivered him to his mother. (Luke 7:11–15)

This incident took place following Jesus' healing of the centurion's servant. He was now on His way out from Capernaum. Nain, given the status of "city" in the narrative, was located in hilly country to the west of the Jordan River, southeast of Nazareth, and about twenty-five miles from Capernaum. But the city itself is not the focus here; Jesus performed this miracle before reaching the city gates.

Jesus was walking toward the city, accompanied by His disciples and a number of other people when their group was intercepted by another crowd—a funeral procession. The group exiting the city would have been marked by the traditional loud, emotional mourners, but the noisemakers were not the ones who drew Jesus' attention. He focused, instead, upon the individual who was genuinely mourning—the widowed mother of the dead man. Notice the text doesn't say that He heard her crying; it says, rather, "When the Lord saw her." I wonder if perhaps the depth of her grief in those moments moving toward her son's burial was so great that no sound escaped from her lips. There are times in life when emotional pain is so immense that one feels the heart must surely and actually break; the pain is too extreme for words or even for sound. Instead, one's entire internal self feels constricted in iron bands, and tears course silently down the cheeks. Surely this occasion was cause for just such painful extremity. The funeral procession represented sorrow upon sorrow: the term *widow* makes that evident. The woman wasn't walking this sad route to the cemetery for the first time. She had taken it in earlier days, as well—when she had followed her husband's bier.

We can know assuredly that the dear woman exited Nain's city gate in great loneliness that day: lingering loneliness for her husband and brutal, raw loneliness for her only son. Whatever the personalities and relationships represented within the group of mourners around her, she walked in sorrow's isolation. Those of us who have followed a loved one's casket know that uniquely isolating reality.

Besides grief, what other burdens did the mourning woman carry? We're not told how long she had been widowed. But her husbandless state had made her vulnerable; his death would have stripped her of financial support. How had she managed to survive, supporting herself and her son? We don't know; surely, though, there would have been emotional and practical struggles involved in eking out a living after her husband died. That wasn't a day when women could easily join the work force to support themselves. Those in her extended family may have stepped in to provide aid, and a few compassionate neighbors also may have contributed occasionally in some way. But to some degree widow-hood would have made her a social dependent. Certainly not a happy picture, is it? None of us likes to be in a position necessitat-ing others helping us.

In the days following her husband's death, there would have been one silver lining in the cloudy sky of her life: she had a son. Though unable to help her significantly while still a child, we're told that at the time of his death he was a "young man." He was coming to or had arrived at the age that he could assume at least part of his mother's care. The days should have been, then, a time of great relief and joy. But not so: the young man had died. The widow's mind surely must have moved beyond the dusty roadway to travel tortured, mazelike paths as she contemplated her future.

Perhaps, too, there was another physical factor involved. We don't know how long the son had been ill, or even whether his death had resulted from illness or accident. Had either a chronic illness or irreversible injuries led to his death, his mother's care of him through weeks or months would have depleted her physical reserves. Such predeath nursing responsibilities also would have drained her financially and emotionally.

Whatever may have preceded the funeral, the woman Jesus saw that day had an enormous need—and He responded with commensurate power. She didn't cry out to Him. She didn't approach Him. She didn't, perhaps, even take note of His presence until He walked up to her and spoke. The woman was wholly bound up in the heartbreaking moment. Knowing her need, Jesus took the initiative. He spoke directly to her hurting heart: "Stop crying." Stop crying! What a shock she must have felt as He spoke those words! Here was a stranger, moving forward from among a crowd of strangers, speaking a command that presented a seeming impossibility. The well of her sorrow was immeasurably deep, and her eyes' flood rose from an internal artesian cavern. He was telling her to do the impossible! Yet perhaps the very jolt of those words stanched her tears.

Then to her astonished eyes came the blessed, incomprehensible sight: Jesus moved to the funeral bier, laid His hand upon it, and its bearers halted. More words were spoken—words of an even more impossible command—"Young man, I say unto thee, Arise" (7:14b).

Instantly, there he was: her precious son, alive! Speaking and perfectly well.

I see in the passage yet another tiny, sweet fact. Look what happened after the young man was loosed from death. The mother didn't rush forward and clasp him to her heart as we'd expect her to do. Instead, she seems to have been frozen by the wonder she beheld. Jesus, the God of the impossible, sealed His conquest of two impossibilities: He presented her son—alive—and He certainly stopped her tears! "And He delivered him to his mother" (7:15b).

The woman had to have been totally overwhelmed by what happened in those few minutes. The day that had begun and progressed as a foot-dragging, leaden-hearted trip to bury her precious son had become a miracle of restored life both for the boy and for her. Her world, which seemed such a short time ago crushed to powder, had instantly become whole and sun-warmed. It was too much to take in, too fantastic for her mind to grasp. There she stood—eyes, ears, and all of self filled with incredulity. So Jesus went that extra step in His compassionate ministering to her: He personally delivered the boy from the bier to her arms.

Jesus' meeting with the widow of Nain took only a matter of minutes. But how beautifully it expresses God's character and His heart. A visit to foreign lands invariably leaves me aching inside as I witness the ugliness of "other gods." Jeremiah long ago recorded Jehovah's mockery of them and their makers:

> For the customs of the people are vain: for one cutteth a tree out of the forest, the work of the hands of the workman, with the axe. They deck it with silver and with gold; they fasten it with nails and with hammers, that it move not. They are upright as the palm tree, but speak not: they must needs be borne, because they cannot go. (Jer. 10:3–5)

Human beings create grotesque gods—not only in form but also in function. Aloof, unpredictable, and demanding, they bind worshipers to them with chains of fear. The worshiper works, worships, and sacrifices to no avail. "For all the gods of the people are idols: but the Lord made the heavens. Glory and honour are in his presence; strength and gladness are in his place" (1 Chron. 16:26–27).

It was that unique creator God Who intercepted the widow's path outside Nain. It was the maker of the heavens Who demonstrated His strength in behalf of her human helplessness.

It is impossible to imagine the widow's joy as she and her son reversed their cemetery route. Yet however great her rejoicing in the marvel of the moment, there must have been great rejoicing in what the moment had shown her of Jehovah. I wonder if perhaps in years to follow her life theme echoed His words recorded in Jeremiah: "Let not the rich man glory in his riches: but let him that glorieth glory in this, that he understandeth and knoweth me, that I am the Lord which exercise lovingkindness, judgment, and righteousness, in the earth" (9:23–24).

Meeting Him with Her

As we have revisited the scene through imagination's lens, what lies within it for our ordinary days and hours? There are one or more "Nain gateway" experiences for us: they are an inevitable part of life.

No one escapes the sorrow of loss. Like the widow of Nain we sooner or later will grieve over the death of a friend or loved one. Removal of that precious person leaves a great pit of loneliness. Of course Jesus doesn't raise our dear ones to life—now. But those individuals who were born-again believers will be raised and returned to us one marvelous day future. While the pangs of sorrow are real and strong, Jesus' "Weep not" prevents despair now and beautifies our tears with hope's rainbow as we look to tomorrow.

Death strikes hopes and dreams, taking them, as well as people, from us. The more strongly held our yearnings are, the more painful their loss is. Yet at that Nain, too, the Lord meets us and responds to our aching hearts. In those instances He may dry our tears by helping us to recognize the dream as being unworthy. Or He may restore its life at another time.

From my earliest years I loved horses. Although there were several times when we had enough acreage to keep a horse, there was no money to do so. I compensated somewhat by riding neighbors' and friends' horses whenever possible. Then when I was ten, my dream crystallized and shone with the brilliance of never-before possibility. Daddy took me to some horse pens located near the tiny railway station in our town. He'd heard that a horse could be bought cheap: they were on their way to the slaughterhouse. The dream therefore took on extra sparkle, since I'd be not only acquiring a horse but also saving it from a sad end. When we got to the horse pens, I walked all around them, carefully looking over each animal—not only from ground level but also from the elevated perspective gained by perching atop the fence. Lest my father totally run out of patience, I settled upon a black-and-white paint gelding. He was about fifteen hands tall, of good conformation and head, and his action in the pen demonstrated a lively but not mean spirit. Then we went home for Daddy to arrange to borrow a truck to transfer the horse and to check out our old corral and barn so the horse could share housing with our milk cow. Throughout the daylight hours my heart floated on clouds of expectancy, and night was filled with dreams of pinto-mounted exploits.

At last, in the borrowed truck and with the $50 purchase price in hand, we returned to the railway siding. But the horse pens were empty. Absolutely empty. "My horse" had gone to the slaughterhouse, and my heart went to sorrow's depths. Shortly thereafter our family moved first to an apple orchard and then to Phoenix, where in either place horse ownership was out of the question.

Years later my long-dead dream was touched to life: I was given not one horse, but two! One was a Tennessee walking horse filly I had the pleasure to break and train by myself. The other was a wonderful white gelding crossbreed: his American saddlebred and Arabian blood made him a spirited, satin-smooth mount. The several years in which I was able to care for, ride, and love those horses were not depleted by the "fallow" years since age ten. Instead, the experience was enriched. As a mature woman with children, I could savor the beauty and joy of horse ownership to a degree that would have been impossible in my preteens.

Other dead dreams are touched to life differently. While growing up in Washington State, I foresaw my future as a time in which I'd have a wonderful opportunity to express my artistic bent while living close to my family. That family relationship was particularly precious to me in terms of my mother and my three siblings. Following God's clear leading to and provision for college training at Bob Jones University however, and subsequent marriage to the third Bob Jones to preside over the school, my dream became considerably reshaped by reality. My "artistic bent" proved unequal to a college major in art. And thousands of miles lie between me and all my other blood relations, who continue to live in Washington. Although I've never painted those imagined minor masterpieces, God has allowed me to "paint" dramatic characters by acting and to "sculpt" stage productions through directing. Despite the fact that I've been able to return to Washington only on rare occasions, the Lord has provided a "family" of wonderful faculty, staff, and students, as well as sisters in Christ in far-flung parts of the globe. Moreover, divine reshaping has marvelously allowed all my grown-up years to be in the context of ministry for the Lord Jesus.

Haven't you, too, found some dream—perhaps a little, private one—dead on a bier, then been amazed as you saw it touched to life by God's great hand?

OUR SELF-SATISFACTION AND SELF-RELIANCE HAVE TO DIE.

Perhaps no one among your family or friends had any idea of that heavenly transaction—that "tiny" miracle—but it was real, and its tenderness ministered enrichment to your heart.

Just as He so graciously undertook for the widow of Nain that long-ago day, so too in our day does He meet us and know and minister.

The widow of Nain was on the same road as Jesus that day so long ago. Otherwise, she never would have met Him, never experienced His personal, miraculous intervention in her life. Moreover, the road's lowest point became its high point. Both of those considerations are true for us as well. Our self-satisfaction and self-reliance have to die. Until those are headed to burial, there can be no raising to life by and in Jesus Christ. "But we had the sentence of death in ourselves, that we should not trust in ourselves, but in God which raiseth the dead: who delivered us from so great a death, and doth deliver: in whom we trust that he will yet deliver us" (2 Cor. 1:9–10).

After our initial meeting with Christ for salvation, we must daily choose to walk the road upon which He is present. Sin's road is dark; salvation's is light. "He that saith he abideth in him ought himself also so to walk, even as he walked" (1 John 2:6).

Satan constantly lures us toward other paths; he doesn't want us to walk in God's light, experiencing and reflecting His presence. We must daily take up the lantern of His Word and step out along the pathway of His will. How precious is His walking with us there!

Even when we faithfully walk the path God chooses for us, there are times when we feel we've missed the way, that we've been abandoned by the Lord. Such a stretch of road, and believers walking it, is shown us in Luke 24. A verse-by-verse examination offers tremendous help for our own "forsaken" stretches on life's road.

> And, behold, two of them went that same day to a village called Emmaus, which was from Jerusalem about three-score furlongs. (v. 13)

As in every story, the setting here is important. "That same day" takes us to earlier verses; we find that this was the first day of the week—but not just an ordinary week's opening day—it was resurrection day. Back in Jerusalem, the tomb in which Jesus had lain was empty; He had conquered death, fulfilling the prophecy of Isaiah 25:8: "He will swallow up death in victory." It was an inexpressibly glorious day, but its news had not reached beyond the city.

The road between Jerusalem and Emmaus was about seven miles long. A short way, really, but it would provide a powerful life lesson for those disciples and for us.

The term "two of them" refers to a pair of believers in Christ. They were not by any means those we've come to think of as key figures. One is not named at all, and the other is identified later as Cleopas. The unfamiliarity underlines their minor roles. Aha! So I—another unimportant, ordinary disciple—feel comfortable stepping onto the road with them. A third figure appears:

> And it came to pass, that, while they communed together and reasoned, Jesus himself drew near, and went with them. (v. 15)

This, of course, is the individual of note in the incident. Who is this One? "Jesus"—the God of eternity inhabiting the time-bound body of a human being, He Who has all power, all wisdom, the ever-sovereign Creator. I love the way the Lord saw to the wording: "Jesus himself"—as if to underline the identity of this third party and to intimate what it should have meant to the two disciples. He didn't send a messenger; He came Himself. In that lies the marvelous difference between Christianity and every religion of the world: the personal living relationship a believer experiences with Jesus Christ.

And what of Jesus' approach? He "drew near." He didn't stand beside the road and shout a greeting or keep a distance between Himself and the disciples that could indicate their great unlikeness. Rather, He drew so close to them they could feel His physical presence; He came into their personal space. He does that for you and me at times, as well, doesn't He? There are moments when the Lord's presence is so real we feel we could almost reach out and touch Him.

But there's more: "and went with them." This wasn't just a fleeting momentary entrance into their walk. He suited His steps to theirs. Imagine what probably characterized those steps: slow, dragging. So the walkers—three of them now—moved on down the dusty roadway together. The addition of that third person should have turned the moment into something glorious, but . . . Now we come to a problem: "But their eyes were holden, that they should not know him" (v. 16).

What? These two were disciples. Think what that word indicates about them. "Disciples" are followers; these two were followers of Jesus. Perhaps they had been with Him throughout all the three and a half years of His earthly ministry. More, they were believers in Him; their hearts had been discipled—they weren't among those who had followed Him just for the excitement or to eat the loaves and fish. As disciples they had been with Him not only through ordinary days of eating, drinking, walking but also in extraordinary days of miracles. Think what they had likely seen the Nazarene do: open blind eyes . . . unstop ears that had never heard a sound . . . speak peace and sanity to demon-ravaged men and women. Yet they didn't know Him there on the road to Emmaus.

> BECAUSE THEY FAILED TO RECOGNIZE JESUS, THEY WALKED ON IN THEIR LONELINESS.

Because they failed to recognize Jesus, they walked on in their loneliness—despite the presence of that One Whose company is closer, warmer, more compassionate than anyone else's could ever be. They walked on in their sadness—though His presence as their risen Lord was cause for joy greater than any they'd ever known. On they walked in their fearfulness—in spite of the fact that moving there with them was their ever-living fortress. They stumbled on toward Emmaus, befuddled and bewildered, unable to partake of their Sovereign's boundless wisdom.

Why? Their failure to recognize Jesus seems really incredible, doesn't it? As Jesus began to talk to them, we come to understand their "holden" eyes. "And he said unto them, What manner of communications are these that ye have one to another, as ye walk, and are sad?" (v. 17).

He of course didn't need to ask. He knew, and we're allowed to know too because of verses 14–15: "And they talked together of all these things which had happened."

Their talking was core to their problem. They were going over and over the events of past days; reiteration only brought greater puzzlement. Back and forth went the words, but their communication with each other was empty of enlightenment. Though they concentrated all their powers of reasoning, they could come up with no answers. Were their mental processes and useless conversations strange or unique? Not at all. We do the same thing time after time and experience similar results. Our talking and reasoning sometimes isn't even oral or directed toward anyone else but instead an inner monologue that is just as defeating. So we walk on as if alone, missing the boundless help available in our Savior as He accompanies us.

It's easy to imagine the contents of the disciples' talk. Even without verses 18–24 in which they go through it all again, we can hear them

~ dwelling on their loss.

~ delving into rational understanding.

~ dismayed in the enormity of emotion.

Verse 21 is particularly powerful in revealing a major factor in their mental maze and emotional quagmire: "But we trusted that it had been he which should have redeemed Israel: and beside all this, to day is the third day since these things were done."

"Things didn't turn out the way we expected! Someone threw us a curve ball! Life's not fair! We've spent all this time believing, and what's it all worth, anyway?" Jesus let them go through their litany of disappointment and complaint, then He spoke again. His words pack an enormous wollop: "O fools, and slow of heart to believe all that the prophets have spoken . . . And beginning at Moses and all the prophets, he expounded unto them in all the scriptures the things concerning himself (vv. 25, 27).

When I read "O fools, and slow of heart," I feel that surely the Lord has said that of and to me over and over again in my years of walking with Him. In fact, "Fool and Slow of Heart" could well be the bold-print framework for my spiritual name tag! How precious is God's longsuffering with us His dusty children.

Now look where Jesus got their foolish minds to focus: on His Word. "And He took them back to Moses"—going over the ABCs of Truth, as it were. That is, of course, where you and I must go when we are puzzled, disappointed, discouraged, sad, fearful . . .

Not only do we find the cure for all of those negatives but our eyes are opened and we see HIM. Renewed awareness of His presence makes the pathway bright. Those glorious changes came to the two disciples on the Emmaus Road the moment they recognized Him.

The roadway near Nain . . . the Emmaus road . . . wherever our life pathway, God intends that it be a place of our learning as we walk in His presence. As we leave the widow of Nain, we can take with us encouragement for every part of our life journey: "And, lo, I am with you alway, even unto the end of the world" (Matt. 28:20*b*).

Jesus Christ is there, in accordance with His promise. Not only does He minister to our now, but He also focuses our hope upon that marvelous day future when He will lay His hand upon death's bier and make it halt forever!

Chapter 6

THE SINFUL ANOINTER

When we think of Jesus having His feet anointed, our mind probably most often goes to the incident when Mary of Bethany performed the act. But there was an earlier occurrence as well. Interesting distinctions can be seen in the two events.

> And one of the Pharisees desired him that he would eat with him. And he went into the Pharisee's house, and sat down to meat. And, behold, a woman in the city, which was a sinner, when she knew that Jesus sat at meat in the Pharisee's house, brought an alabaster box of ointment, and stood at his feet behind him weeping, and began to wash his feet with tears, and did wipe them with the hairs of her head, and kissed his feet, and anointed them with the ointment. (Luke 7:36–38)

It seems strange to us that anyone, especially a woman of the streets, could or would intrude upon a meal in a private home, as in this instance. But in those non-TV, non–game room, pre-DVD days, entertainment came in different forms. Anything considered an event could draw curious onlookers. This woman probably was not the only uninvited person. But she certainly was the only one who did what she did.

The sect of Pharisees in Jewry as a whole were constant and loud in their opposition to Jesus. Those hidebound, self-righteous religionists detested Him and the menace He represented to their spiritual stranglehold upon the people. Yet Jesus did not refuse the dinner invitation made by an individual Pharisee.

I wonder if perhaps the supper's location itself gave the woman boldness to enter the house and perform her act. That is, she likely would have avoided a setting in which all but she were followers of Jesus. The Pharisee's house was more neutral ground and not so forbidding. Nevertheless, it could not have been easy for her to intrude upon the scene that evening. The context indicates that she was a recognizable woman of ill repute, but she was so magnetized by whatever she had heard and seen of Jesus that she thrust herself among the invited dinner guests.

How had she heard of the supper? How did she get into the house? We might surmise that both were through the gossip and assistance of household servants; it's hardly credible that any of the Pharisee's own family members or associates would have had direct social contact with such a woman. Whatever the means by which she came, come she did. And she came with purpose. Her motivation was not just curiosity to see Jesus. She made her way to the house and into the room with two things that were precious: a sin-weary, yearning heart and an alabaster container of ointment.

The woman took a position behind Jesus' feet as He reclined at the table. She would have been kneeling; the table-side couches were low. Hence, she came to Jesus humbly. It seems to me her intention was simply to apply the ointment to His feet. But something prevented that happening right away: she broke into tears. She wept so unrestrainedly that her tears wet His feet and she had to dry them with her free-flowing hair. That free-flowing hair, by the way, was a badge of her profession as a prostitute. But this poor soul went beyond weeping and wiping; she covered Jesus' feet with kisses. And, last, she applied the ointment to His feet. What a beautiful picture of sorrow for sin and love for the Savior!

But the Pharisee saw no beauty. He saw, first, a shocking act by a socially and religiously unacceptable individual. And, second, he saw his guest's acceptance of her act. Both appalled him. "Now when the Pharisee which had bidden him saw it, he spake within himself, saying, This man, if he were a prophet, would have known who and what manner of woman this is that toucheth him: for she is a sinner" (7:39).

Notice, first, that the Pharisee didn't have the courage to speak. But the swish of his spiritual garments was almost audible as he whirled them away in horror. And of course Jesus heard his revulsion loud and clear. "And Jesus answering said unto him, Simon, I have somewhat to say unto thee" (7:40*a*). I love the word *answering* in that sentence. In the presence of the all-knowing God-man the Pharisee might as well have shouted his objection! But then he quickly attempted an about-face. His oral response came out all warmth, admiration, and interest: "And he saith, Master, say on" (7:40*b*).

As He did so often, Jesus used a story rather than either a direct reproach or preaching. Stories have great power to capture attention and deliver a message. So it was with the one the Lord told that evening.

> There was a certain creditor which had two debtors: the one owed five hundred pence, and the other fifty. And when they had nothing to pay, he frankly forgave them both. Tell me therefore, which of them will love him most? (7:41–42)

The Pharisee was probably relieved to turn his attention to the story and away from what he considered the disgusting scene at his table. And of course the answer to Jesus' query was obvious: "Simon answered and said, I suppose that he, to whom he forgave most" (7:43*a*). No doubt pleased with himself, Simon waited for what would follow—perhaps a little homily on alms-giving or loving one's neighbor or . . . Instead, Jesus brought the Pharisee right back to the present unsettling situation there in his house.

> And he said unto him, Thou hast rightly judged. And he turned to the woman, and said unto Simon, Seest thou this woman? I entered into thine house, thou gavest me no water for my feet: but she hath washed my feet with tears, and wiped them with the hairs of her head. Thou gavest me no kiss: but this woman since the time I came in hath not ceased to kiss my feet. My head with oil thou didst not anoint: but this woman hath anointed my feet with ointment. Wherefore I say unto thee, Her sins, which are many, are forgiven; for she loved much: but to whom little is forgiven, the same loveth little. (7:43*b*–47)

Notice that Jesus briefly acknowledged His host's correct response to the illustration. But Simon had no chance to preen because his guest went on to make the point of His story unmissable through the woman at His feet—a living example. Even the thick layers of self-righteous law-keeping, self-conscious alms-giving, and self-exalting adherence to religious minutiae could not protect the Pharisee from the stab of truth. He, in his momentary and skeptical attention upon the Lord, fell far short of the lowly woman and her love.

Having corrected Simon's acidic view of the moment, Jesus again directed His attention to the anointer and her aromatic act. "And he said unto her, Thy sins are forgiven. And they that sat at meat with him began to say within themselves, Who is this that forgiveth sins also? And he said to the woman, Thy faith hath saved thee: go in peace" (7:48–50).

Scripture does not record a word spoken by the woman; she's just pictured kneeling there at the feet of the Master in total, concentrated worship. Although she was silent, the petition of her heart communicated itself clearly to Jesus, and He graciously granted it. Chills come in imagining the woman's response to those words, "Thy sins are forgiven." To her, *sins* had to be much more than just a term. Jesus had earlier indicated the depths to which she had sunk when He said to the Pharisee, "Her sins, which are many . . ." We don't know how long the woman had lived in the shadows. We're told nothing of specific sins she'd likely committed in her degraded state—lying, stealing, prostitution, drunkenness. The list must have been long indeed. I see her head snap up as she heard those blessed words of forgiveness. Surely her eyes flew from Jesus' feet to His face as she thrilled with the release and joy sweeping through her.

While she exulted in the wonder of her cleansing, the onlookers wondered, too, but questioned how such words could come from human lips. They were steeped in the history of their people, with animal sacrifices demanded by Jehovah for His forgiveness. Yet here, in the home of a Pharisee rather than in the temple, here far from an altar and with no sacrificial animal in view, Jesus declared a sin-stained woman forgiven.

Can't you just see that dear soul frozen there on her knees, her eyes wide in mingled thrill, disbelief, and awe? Jesus tenderly addressed her again, as if to release her from the shocked incomprehension binding her and to confirm the fact of her cleansing. "Thy faith hath saved thee; go in peace" (7:50).

Her faith? Would you or I have interpreted this woman's silent actions that evening as faith? Wouldn't we have expected or demanded words from her? Not so with Jesus. Her heart had declared its belief. She spoke in her tears, in the kisses she lavished on His feet, and in the sacrificial gift of the precious ointment with which she anointed His travel-weary feet.

Everyone else in Simon's house had some attitude or agenda during the mealtime: superiority, skepticism, uncertainty, curiosity, disbelief, enmity, desire to disprove. The sin-burdened woman simply wanted to be as close to Jesus as she could get. Kneeling there she lavished not only the alabaster-encased ointment but also her soul upon Him. When she went from the room, the alabaster jar was empty of its treasure, but her full soul rejoiced at being made precious through her faith in the Lord Jesus.

Meeting Him with Her

The depth of sinfulness in which this woman lived may seem extreme to some of us who were saved as children. To others, though, who stayed on the unsaved side of the cross well into adulthood, the burden of such sins may be easily remembered. We need to approach this incident recognizing that sin is sin and that Scripture indicates that sins of the spirit—which we handily discount—are equally hateful in God's sight. It comes down to a basic: black is black. Yes, each of us can enter the scene with this woman, humbly admitting that we are her spiritual sisters. If we look upon her from some imagined spiritual elevation, we more accurately resemble Simon the Pharisee.

A woman's tears can be precious things. They certainly were in this incident. The poor soul wept over her sin: without saying a word she expressed her heart's wretchedness. At the feet of the sinless Savior she repented of the sin that had blackened her life. Whatever the public knew of her by reputation, she knew as degraded, hateful reality. Jesus spoke blessed cleansing of her sin. So, too, for you and me: "Now ye are clean through the word which I have spoken unto you" (John 15:3).

Honest acknowledgment of sin figures large in genuine salvation: we must know ourselves to be dead in our sins in order to come to life in Jesus Christ.

Beyond the tears of our own initial repentance, how recently have we wept over dirtying our precious garments of salvation? Christ's blood weaves for us a beautiful robe of righteousness. "I will greatly rejoice in the Lord, my soul shall be joyful in my God; for he hath clothed me with the garments of salvation, he hath covered me with the robe of righteousness" (Isa. 61:10*a*).

So often we let it get bedraggled, ripped, dirt-smeared, and muddy because of where and how we've worn it. Ongoing sins should cause us to weep in repentance too. But do they? Oh, that our hearts might express the repentant agony this dear woman demonstrated.

Because she made Jesus' feet so wet with her crying, the woman used her hair to dry them. She wiped away the wetness with the physical badge of her defilement—and Jesus didn't flinch, pull away, or reprove her. He showed Himself—as ever—the friend of sinners. Glorious thought! Were He anything else, you and I would have been rejected in our plea for salvation's cleansing through His blood. We would have been abandoned in disgust years ago because of our ongoing sins. But praise His dear name, He is ever the friend who sticks closer than any brother.

> Henceforth I call you not servants; for the servant knoweth not what his lord doeth: but I have called you friends; for all things that I have heard of my Father I have made known unto you. (John 15:15)

How faithfully do we emulate Jesus' spirit as it's so clearly shown in this anointing incident? Our hearts are to yearn toward the unsaved people around us—no matter how unlovely—with the desire that they come to know Jesus Christ. This miserable woman was drawn to Jesus—the embodiment of love—not to those who embodied judgmentalism.

DO WE WALK WITH THE LORD IN SUCH A WAY THAT WE'RE ABLE TO SENSE HEART NEEDS OF THOSE AROUND US?

Having washed and dried the Savior's feet, the woman broke the alabaster vessel containing the ointment. The container may have quite closely resembled the one used later by Mary of Bethany. Considering the chasm of difference between the two women, the ointment containers represent tremendous difference in terms of their probable acquirement. Mary, being a mature, pure single woman living with her sister, probably received her ointment flask as a gift from a family member or from someone in her circle of friends. By contrast, the woman in this story either had gotten it as a gift in one of her illicit relationships or purchased it with profits from whatever unsavory dealings she had been engaged in.

A difference of origin so great in those two containers might make us recoil from the one in the hands of the streetwalker. Too, the hands holding the container and applying the ointment may have been none too clean. Jesus' recognition of the heart behind the hands should strike us with conviction both in our attitude toward others and in our heart toward Him. Do we walk with the Lord in such a way that we're able to sense heart needs of those around us? Or do we move through life dismissively, untouched by any but our own concerns? Are we aware that our own hands are never entirely clean? That sins persistently cling to them? Does the heart behind the hands faithfully hold them out to Christ for the cleansing only He can give? On that long-ago day in the Pharisee's house the Lord not only accepted the ill-gained gift and the sin-laden giver, He also in turn released her from sin's bondage, turning her sorrow to joy, her degradation to exaltation, her misery to magnificence. May each of us recall our own day of release from condemnation and determine to be more lavish in our love for our blessed Redeemer.

Chapter 7

THE WOMAN WITH AN ISSUE OF BLOOD

Once again three of the four Gospel writers saw fit to record a time when Jesus touched and changed a woman's life. Read carefully through the passages below.

> And behold, a woman, which was diseased with an issue of blood twelve years, came behind him, and touched the hem of his garment. For she said within herself, If I may but touch his garment, I shall be whole. But Jesus turned him about, and when he saw her, he said, Daughter, be of good comfort; thy faith hath made thee whole. And the woman was made whole from that hour. (Matt. 9:20–22)

> And a certain woman, which had an issue of blood twelve years, and had suffered many things of many physicians, and had spent all that she had, and was nothing bettered, but rather grew worse, when she had heard of Jesus, came in the press behind, and touched his garment. For she said, If I may touch but his clothes, I shall be whole. And straightway the fountain of her blood was dried up; and she felt in her body that she was healed of that plague. And Jesus, immediately knowing in

himself that virtue had gone out of him, turned him about in the press, and said, Who touched my clothes? And his disciples said unto him, Thou seest the multitude thronging thee, and sayest thou, Who touched me? And he looked round about to see her that had done this thing. But the woman fearing and trembling, knowing what was done in her, came and fell down before him, and told him all the truth. And he said unto her, Daughter, thy faith hath made thee whole; go in peace, and be whole of thy plague. (Mark 5:25–34)

And a woman having an issue of blood twelve years, which had spent all her living upon physicians, neither could be healed of any, came behind him, and touched the border of his garment: and immediately her issue of blood stanched. And Jesus said, Who touched me? When all denied, Peter and they that were with him said, Master, the multitude throng thee and press thee, and sayest thou, Who touched me? And Jesus said, Somebody hath touched me: for I perceive that virtue is gone out of me. And when the woman saw that she was not hid, she came trembling, and falling down before him, she declared unto him before all the people for what cause she had touched him, and how she was healed immediately. And he said unto her, Daughter, be of good comfort: thy faith hath made thee whole; go in peace. (Luke 8:43–48)

This needy woman interrupted one of Jesus' ministry trips. He and His disciples were going with Jairus to raise the synagogue ruler's daughter from death. On the way a desperate woman claimed Jesus' attention.

What a fascinating juxtaposition of life situations appears here: the Master was on His way to help a twelve-year-old girl; His going was delayed by a mature woman who had agonized with a physical problem for twelve years. She had suffered the equivalent of the girl's entire life span! Jairus's daughter had been enjoying some of life's happiest, most carefree years; the woman had endured an equal number of years filled with some of the worst suffering a woman can know.

And what suffering. How many times have you read these accounts and gone lightly over the description given—"an issue of blood"—without considering the real meaning of the phrase? As women, you and I can recognize the awfulness contained in those simple words and identify with the desperation that drove her to Jesus. This was a chronic female condition that would have profoundly affected every part of her world.

Think first of the physical consequences: she was, in effect, enduring nonstop menstruation. Any one of us can at least imagine to some degree the complications created by having "menstrual period" (days) translate into menstrual years. There are physical factors connected to and resulting from the human female menstrual cycle: outstandingly, the reduction of iron available for the body, which can result in an overall rundown condition. Multiply that once-a-month effect by twelve years of blood loss! Consider, too, the likely discomfort that was part of her malady—menstrual cramps. Nor did she have access to specially designed feminine products to ease her difficulty. Poor woman! It was as if her entire physiology had betrayed her, had become her enemy.

Or think about the emotional aspect. Her physical abnormality would have been unavoidably apparent to her no matter what her IQ. Her mother, sisters, and friends who knew of her freakish state would surely express dismay and offer all sorts of suggestions for help or cure. We women suffer emotionally in those areas of life where we consider ourselves below par or strange. How much stranger could she have been thought than in having such a basic flaw in her feminine structure and function? The normal menstrual period is a time of heightened awareness, sensitivity, and a tendency toward embarrassment. How greatly those emotional realities would have been increased through the longevity of the flow this poor woman endured. Instead of the normal five-to-seven days once a month with recovery and normalcy between periods, her condition lasted approximately four thousand, three hundred eighty days! More emotionally traumatic yet would have been the fact that she had to consult physicians—all of whom would have been male—about her intimate suffering. Both her feminine makeup and the day's cultural norms would have made such consultations extremely difficult. What horrors might their recommendations and treatments have meant? Medical practice in that era embraced some near-brutalities.

Although her problem was of the most intimate sort, it surely had relational and social consequences as well. When a woman of those times was experiencing "the way of women," she was considered unclean. She could not know sexual intimacy with her husband; she was, to a certain degree, set apart from normal social activity. Spiritually, too, she was an outcast. Her physical condition kept her from worship. Essentially she must have felt like a leper. Although her "leprosy" was invisible, it bound her heart in cords of pain, and it presented a cruel barrier against normal living.

Finally, we learn in the narrative that the twelve years of her malady had stripped her of money. Though she had endured the mortifying embarrassment of relating her troubles to male doctors, consultation after consultation left her condition worsening and her finances depleted. This pitiable soul was in desperate straits spiritually, physically, emotionally, socially, and financially.

That desperation drove her out into the crowd that swarmed the Nazarene wherever He went. That desperation made her put aside embarrassment to work her way through the masses of people who likewise wanted to get near Him. Yet the desperation driving her was not despair—her words reveal that it was fueled by faith.

We don't know how the woman heard of Jesus. We know nothing of the number of times she heard or how long it took her to come to believe in His powers. Apparently she alone in her circle of relationships had the kind of faith she demonstrated that day, for the Scripture indicates she was alone in her attempt to reach Jesus. Unlike Jairus's daughter, she had no one who cared enough to intercede for her.

There is something particularly beautiful in this dear woman's approach to Jesus. First, there is the tremendous humility of her faith. She did not approach Him boldly or in any kind of strength. As befitting her socially outcast state, she moved in behind Him and bent down to seek some trailing portion of His garment. This woman didn't feign humility—she was thoroughly and genuinely humble.

There is a second aspect of beauty in the seeker's coming to Jesus that day: the littleness of her silent petition. She defied social restrictions; she battled her way alone through the crowd. Yet she sought such tiny contact with the Nazarene. Verbal petitions were many throughout the days of Jesus' earthly ministry, and the words sought great help: restoration of sight or hearing or mobility. But this woman, amazingly, sought only to make contact with the edge of His garment.

Of course that tentative touch did not escape Jesus' notice. Out of all the jostling and jockeying bodies on every side, He sensed a different touch: the whisper of fingers barely brushing His garment. Note how Scripture indicates Jesus' awareness: "Immediately knowing in himself that virtue had gone out of him" (Mark 5:30*b*).

That description gives us reason to marvel and rejoice anew at Christ's giving of Himself to us in our relationship to Him. This dear woman expected only a distanced demonstration of Jesus' power; she experienced the blessed reality of His personal involvement.

That touch of humble faith received its reward: the awful flow of blood stopped instantly. But Jesus did more than heal her physical malady. He stopped in His progress to Jairus's house, stopped all of the disciples and the hangers-on, stopped to meet the need of a woman whose problem was such a private, intimate devastation. He called her forth, and she stood trembling before Him. As He had already ministered to her body, so now too He ministered to her soul. Notice His form of address to her: "Daughter" (5:34*b*).

I can barely imagine the great tenderness communicated by that pronunciation. His attitude of warm acceptance was so unlike what she had experienced from others in those twelve long years. Throughout those years human beings had shunned her, horrified by her condition. God in human flesh welcomed her, compassionate toward her suffering. Jesus' spirit and words gave her the courage to stand forth, to tell the secret suffering she had endured—and that she was cured when she touched Him. Now notice a word Mark used in his narrative: he says that Jesus told the woman, "Be whole of thy plague" (5:34*c*).

The Son of God did not minimize the tortuously intimate need she brought to Him. He knew the devastating effects it had wrought in her world. Those around her might consider it minimal in comparison to the blindness, deafness, and crippling that others endured. People in general might have thought hers such an unspeakable malady that it should not be brought to the healer. Not so Jesus Christ. He recognized the sweeping effects of her female condition: it was, indeed, a plague. He Who had created the female body knew the intricacies and effects of its functioning, knew that the long malfunctioning had wounded her spirit. "The spirit of a man will sustain his infirmity; but a wounded spirit, who can bear?" (Prov. 18:14).

She crept up shamefully behind Him, battered by a private plague. She went from Him healed in body, honored by His public response, and at peace in her soul.

$\mathcal{M}$EETING HIM WITH HER

This woman's story strikes me first with the length of her suffering. Life's brief periods of difficulty, while not easy or pleasurable, are more readily endured than those that linger. The longer a burdensome experience drags on, the more the sufferer is tempted to despair. Certainly twelve years of menstrual flow ranks high in such a category. But this woman chose faith over despair. What an admirable choice! And how it challenges me. Time is a weighty factor in suffering of any kind: when "endless" enters one's thinking, endurance may seem impossible. Twelve years surely would have made the sense of endlessness such an integral part of her experience that it accompanied each beat of her heart. Nevertheless, she steeled herself against understandable despair and chose admirable, determined faith—faith that took her to Jesus and thus to healing. What a pity that "hopeless" so often rises to stand as a barricade against one's going to Christ.

> Is there no balm in Gilead; is there no physician there? why
> then is not the health of the daughter of my people recovered?
> (Jer. 8:22)

We know that Scripture consistently urges us to faith. Yet sometimes even our faith itself becomes a deterrent to our seeking the Lord. That happens when we measure its size or classify it in terms of strength. The woman with the issue of blood obviously didn't have a big faith, but a small one. She didn't have a bold faith, but a timid one. The size and spirit of her faith are evident in her tentative touch upon the trailing edge of Jesus' garment. And yet it was enough. She probably discounted it; He didn't. Hers was that tiny, mustard-seed-like faith Jesus at another time commended, promising that great things can result from it—not because of our faith's deserving but because of God's power in response to our call. "Verily I say unto you, If ye have faith as a grain of mustard seed, ye shall say unto this mountain, Remove hence to yonder place; and it shall remove; and nothing shall be impossible unto you" (Matt. 17:20).

The next thing that leaps from this Bible narrative in terms of speaking to our day is the intimate nature of the woman's need. I believe our era of Christianity suffers with spiritual anemia in part because of intimate feminine sins. A woman's smiling Sunday face may mask a self whose Monday walls enclose furtive indulgences. The subjects mentioned in this section are such that I would prefer not to handle them, but they need to be exposed. Pretending they don't exist in our circles just worsens our spiritual ill health.

First, let's turn the light on intimate sins that are primarily physical.

Drug dependency. The drugs a woman uses may be prescription or over the counter. Many times the beginning usage comes in response to a physical problem: pain or sleeplessness or depression . . . The sufferer went to a drugstore or a doctor for help. But the intended temporary assistance has become a permanent dependence.

Alcohol dependency. Whether it's wine or hard liquor, the woman cleverly disguises her intake and hides her supply.

Smoking. Although she knows the much-publicized evidence of smoking's harmfulness, the Christian woman smoker continues in her nicotine dependence.

Food dependency. When thoughts return repeatedly to food, when food intake is too frequent and too abundant, when food is used as an emotional cure—all of those indicate food dependency. The Bible calls it gluttony.

Although she may feign biblical obedience, the hidden, intimate sins just named not only keep a woman enslaved but also defile her body, the temple of the Holy Spirit.

Masturbation. Whether single or married, the woman excuses her secret practice of self-induced orgasm, claiming it to be harmless because it's neither fornication nor adultery. This particular practice may have started in childhood, with years of indulgence making it seem inescapable. But it is not harmless: unclean imagination is part of masturbation. Nor is its conquest beyond Christ's power.

Because the last-named covert sin clearly joins the body with the mind, it can serve as a bridge into intimate mental sins.

Fantasizing. Hour after hour behind the walls of her home a woman may move far beyond those walls to create another persona or world where she can indulge herself. Modernity assists her via daytime TV, DVDs, virtual reality, online chat rooms, pornographic telephone sources, and so forth. Though there are of course varying degrees of involvement, persistent fantasizing is sin because it denies reality and opens the mind to darkness.

Gambling. God's way to financial supply is work. Not so a gambler. Always hoping for a "lucky break," she enthrones chance as her god. There is also a form of gambling that excludes cards, machines, or lottery tickets: overspending. The woman who buys beyond budgetary limits gambles that her extravagance will remain undiscovered and that income will somehow increase to cover the overage.

Entertainment addiction. This is an area in which an enormous number of Christian women seem trapped. Whether it's romance novels, TV in general, computer communication and games, or a particular show "I just can't miss," God's gift of time is sacrificed on the altar of personal pleasure.

The very fact of their being secret contributes to a woman's continuing in her intimate sin. There is excitement in a "me alone" world. In Proverbs 9:17 the foolish woman states, "Stolen waters are sweet, and bread eaten in secret is pleasant."

She is foolish indeed, denying or ignoring the psalmist's riveting acknowledgment to God: "Thou has set our iniquities before thee; our secret sins in the light of thy countenance (Ps. 90:8).

Proverbs 21:17 applies to tightly clutched intimate sins: "He that loveth pleasure shall be a poor man: he that loveth wine and oil shall not be rich."

The impoverishment mentioned is not just a matter of dollars and cents; life worth itself is drained away by addictions. Even more basic is the fact that an addiction or dependency displaces God. If you are one who continues to harbor an intimate sin, please recognize your violation of the very first of God's laws: "Thou shalt have no other gods before me" (Exod. 20:3). Choosing another god by holding on to intimate sins deprives the believer of precious riches: unsullied fellowship with the Lord Jesus.

It is sad to think of Christian women practicing any of the above "intimate" sins. Why do they allow these things in their life? They choose to do so because there is a sense of relief, of escape, of reality's harsh edges being softened. They consider such "little" things to be too ingrained to be dealt with. Some no doubt have, like the woman with her issue of blood, sought human help. Where there was no enlistment of divine help, there of course was failure—perhaps multiple failures. Like the woman who sought to touch the hem of Jesus' garment, any woman bound by cords of intimate sin needs to make her way to Jesus Christ, bow before Him with her tiny faith, reach out to Him, and experience deliverance from her enslavement.

> TO HOLD GOD AT ARMS' LENGTH, SO TO SPEAK, IS TO MISS UNIMAGINABLE SPIRITUAL RICHES.

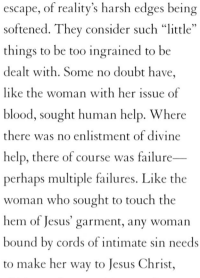

Jesus stated the binding power of these sins in John 8:34—"Verily, verily, I say unto you, Whosoever committeth sin is the servant of sin."

Finally, do we qualify our needs, reserving some as too personal, too intimate to take to God in prayer? What could possibly have been more personal or intimate than this woman's awful physical malfunction? Our heavenly Father not only knows every detail of who we are and where we are in life but also delights in our having a relationship with Him so warm that we readily confide our inmost thoughts. To hold God at arms' length, so to speak, is to miss unimaginable spiritual riches. His private, deeply personal workings convey unique delight. "Unspoken prayer requests" should be a phrase applied only in our horizontal relationships—never in our all-important vertical one. We know Philippians 4:6 in our head, but it needs to be transferred to our heart and become active there: "Be careful for nothing; but in every thing by prayer and supplication with thanksgiving let your requests be made known unto God."

May each of us more consistently move forward to touch the hem of Christ's garment so that He can free us from our intimate maladies of mind and heart.

Chapter 8

JAIRUS'S DAUGHTER

A very young woman Jesus encountered during His life here on earth is mentioned in three of the four Gospels—the daughter of Jairus. See her as she's presented book by book.

> While he spake these things unto them, behold, there came
> a certain ruler, and worshipped him, saying, My daughter
> is even now dead: but come and lay thy hand upon her, and
> she shall live. And Jesus arose, and followed him, and so did
> his disciples. . . . And when Jesus came into the ruler's house,
> and saw the minstrels and the people making a noise, he said
> unto them, Give place: for the maid is not dead, but sleepeth.
> And they laughed him to scorn. But when the people were put
> forth, he went in and took her by the hand, and the maid arose.
> (Matt. 9:18–19, 23–25)

> And when Jesus was passed over again by ship unto the other
> side, much people gathered unto him: and he was nigh unto
> the sea. And, behold, there cometh one of the rulers of the
> synagogue, Jairus by name; and when he saw him, he fell at
> his feet. And besought him greatly, saying, My little daughter

lieth at the point of death: I pray thee, come and lay thy hands on her, that she may be healed; and she shall live. And Jesus went with him; and much people followed him, and thronged him. . . . While he yet spake, there came from the ruler of the synagogue's house certain which said, Thy daughter is dead: why troublest thou the Master any further? As soon as Jesus heard the word that was spoken, he saith unto the ruler of the synagogue, Be not afraid, only believe. And he suffered no man to follow him, save Peter, and James, and John the brother of James. And he cometh to the house of the ruler of the synagogue, and seeth the tumult, and them that wept and wailed greatly. And when he was come in, he saith unto them, Why make ye this ado, and weep? the damsel is not dead, but sleepeth. And they laughed him to scorn. But when he had put them all out, he taketh the father and the mother of the damsel, and them that were with him, and entereth in where the damsel was lying. And he took the damsel by the hand, and said unto her, Talitha cumi, which is, being interpreted, Damsel, I say unto thee, arise. (Mark 5:21–24, 35–42)

And it came to pass, that, when Jesus was returned, the people gladly received him: for they were all waiting for him. And, behold, there came a man named Jairus, and he was a ruler of the synagogue: and he fell down at Jesus' feet, and besought him that he would come into his house: for he had one only daughter, about twelve years of age, and she lay a dying. But as he went the people thronged him. . . . While he yet spake, there cometh one from the ruler of the synagogue's house, saying to him, Thy daughter is dead; trouble not the Master. But when Jesus heard it, he answered him, saying, Fear not: believe only, and she shall be made whole. And when he came into the house, he suffered no man to go in, save Peter and James, and John, and the father and the mother of the maiden. And all wept, and bewailed her: but he said, Weep not; she is not dead, but sleepeth. And they laughed him to scorn, knowing that she was dead. And he put them all out, and took her by the hand, and called, saying, Maid, arise. And her spirit came again, and she arose straightway: and he commanded to give her meat. (Luke 8:40–42, 49–55)

Notice that in this incident we witness Jesus' contact with someone at the early end of life's spectrum: a girl of twelve just coming into the bloom of womanhood. Her story follows those of considerably older women who crossed Jesus' path: Anna, the Samaritan woman, Peter's mother-in-law, the sinful woman who anointed His feet, and the woman with the issue of blood.

Jesus met the girl's need—not because of her own faith or petition but because of her father's intercession. "Jairus's daughter" is the nearest we come to a name, yet there's a good deal we can determine other than her given age. First, we see that although she was not yet in her teens, she enjoyed a certain social status through her parentage: her father was a ruler of the local synagogue. He would have been respected and admired by the Jewish community, with his family sharing in his recognition. His standing among his people is inferred, in part, by the number of friends who gathered to worry, weep, and wail for his daughter.

Beyond being somewhat special in the community, this girl was obviously special in her family: she was Jairus's only daughter. Bonding between daughters and fathers is naturally strong; that bond in the case of an only child may be greatly intensified. Something of the strength of their relationship can be seen in at least three aspects of the incident we're considering. First, there is the fact that Jairus went to Jesus at all; doing so may have jeopardized his standing with his spiritual peers. Second, he sought the Nazarene himself rather than sending his wife or a servant. And third, the manner in which he presented his petition shouts his paternal heart burden. Right there in the crowd, with curious locals—some of whom he had probably taught—looking on, he dropped to his knees, mindless of both his social position and his spiritual office.

Established religion of the day did not take well to Jesus the Nazarene; in fact, most of what He said went against all they had come to hold dear. As is the case today, there was a herd mentality operative in religious circles: grown-up peer pressure. Jairus no doubt had friends inside and outside the synagogue who personally opposed Jesus and who urged their compatriots to do likewise. But love for his daughter and belief (probably secret to that point) in Jesus' power drove the agonizing father to seek Him out. Thus he boldly took sides against his peers.

Mark's account highlights an interesting aspect of Jairus's appeal. He clearly states his belief when he says, "And she shall live." Only a few lines further along in the passage Jesus challenged him: "Be not afraid, only believe." Between Jairus's statement and Jesus' challenge lay a distressing occurrence: servants had come to tell Jairus the beloved girl had died. Faith in Jesus' healing the sick is one thing, but faith in His raising the dead is something far different! The poor, distressed father no doubt struggled to maintain his grip on belief. Think, too, how the mocking of the mourners must have further pummeled Jairus's heart.

It's instructive to realize how important Jairus's faith was in the situation. His, apparently, was all the faith being exercised in the crisis. The twelve-year-old girl was unable to help herself or ask for help. There is no indication of faith on the part of her mother. Her father undertook for her, stating her desperate need to the Man of Galilee and indicating his own belief in Jesus' power. Notice how immediately Jesus responded: he started toward Jairus's house at once. When He arrived and drove the crowd of mourners from the room, the girl was still unable to make any personal appeal: she was dead. But of course the need was unmistakable: her young life had been snuffed out by humanity's great enemy, death. Although those attending the girl's deathbed considered her to be beyond all hope and help, He Who is Himself life effortlessly overcame the enemy. He took the death-chilled little hand in His. He told her, simply, to get up. And she returned to life.

The warm, strong father-daughter bond implied in the incident must have been tremendously enhanced by the experience of Jesus' raising the girl to life. Surely a father and daughter who had shared that unique experience would have moved on through life expanding their relationship with each other. There is special blessedness in having children grow into friendship with their parents. If ever there were reason for such transitioning, it would have been true for Jairus and his daughter. We would hope that she and her father also demonstrated lifelong faithfulness to Jesus Christ, her life-giver.

We're not told anything of this girl's life following this dramatic incident. But considering the faith her father demonstrated before experiencing the miracle, and knowing him, as a leader in the synagogue, to be well versed in the Scriptures, we can certainly hope that Jairus and his whole house came to the saving knowledge of Christ. It is difficult to imagine that a girl who experienced release from death ever could have forgotten the miracle or lived to bring shame upon Him Who had performed it.

*M*EETING HIM WITH HER

Although none of us has ever experienced the extremity of Jairus's daughter in her illness and death, I believe there are times when we're in situations that parallel hers. That is, we find ourselves in some difficulty or facing some challenge so sudden or so great that we're reduced to occasional brief, whispered pleas for God's help. At such junctures He moves someone to undertake for us in earnest, sustained prayer. Through the years I've known a number of such times: a call or note arrives saying in essence, "God laid you on my heart. I don't know why, but I've been praying for you in a special way." How wonderful! Like Jairus's daughter, our helplessness motivates someone to undertake for us.

Such times of receiving strategic intercessory help should also encourage us to provide it for others as the Lord prompts us to do so.

RECEIVING STRATEGIC INTERCESSORY HELP SHOULD ALSO ENCOURAGE US TO PROVIDE IT FOR OTHERS.

This girl who had her life restored owed a great deal to her biological father. If he had not gone to Jesus with word of her need, she would never have known His resurrecting touch. Thus, he who had given her physical life also made possible her restoration to life. She certainly owed her father honor and gratitude. How about you and me? We owe our physical life to a human father and mother. Do we rightly honor them as God's Word tells us to do? "Honour thy father and thy mother: that thy days may be long upon the land" (Exod. 20:12).

Or do we exempt ourselves on the basis of a parent's being somehow unfit or unworthy of honor? Look again at the command: the very first one God pronounced regarding our horizontal relationships. It does not allow for exemptions. There are even stronger Scripture statements on the subject in Proverbs. "He that wasteth his father, and chaseth away his mother, is a son that causeth shame, and bringeth reproach (19:26).

For many women reading this book, honor for father or mother is easy and natural. But for some it is exceedingly difficult. Parental "unfitness for honor" takes various forms:

~ abandonment

~ neglect

~ betrayal

~ abuse

~ ungodliness

In such cases, not choosing resentment and bitterness in favor of choosing forgiveness and obedient filial honor may be a major spiritual victory. I know that to be true from personal experience.

Jairus's daughter owed every succeeding day of her life to Jesus. But isn't that equally true for us? The psalmist reminds us of our being's real source:

> For thou hast possessed my reins, thou hast covered me in my mother's womb. I will praise thee; for I am fearfully and wonderfully made: marvellous are thy works; and that my soul knoweth right well. My substance was not hid from thee, when I was made in secret, and curiously wrought in the lowest parts of the earth. Thine eyes did see my substance, yet being unperfect; and in thy book all my members were written, which in continuance were fashioned, when as yet there was none of them. (Ps. 139:13–16)

Forgetfulness in Jairus's daughter seems unthinkably awful. That, surely, is one of the important personal applications of her story for you and me. No matter at what age we received the miracle of eternal life through God's Son, Jesus Christ, we should never forget or downplay the miracle, never bring shame upon the name of that mighty One Who has raised us to eternal life with Him. Sadly the opposite is true: too many times we Christians grow spiritually forgetful; we betray the new birth by reverting to the old life. We live so heedlessly that the reputation of our life-giving God is tarnished. Unsaved people see our ugly hypocrisy instead of His beautiful life giving.

> Blessed be the God and Father of our Lord Jesus Christ, who hath blessed us with all spiritual blessings in heavenly places in Christ: according as he hath chosen us in him before the foundation of the world, that we should be holy and without blame before him in love. (Eph. 1:3–4)

Chapter 9

THE CANAANITE WOMAN

In exploring the incidents of Jesus' interactions with women, we've seen His quick and compassionate responses. Now as we move into the second half of the sixteen recorded meetings, we find something so different it seems shocking.

> Then Jesus went thence, and departed into the coasts of Tyre and Sidon. And, behold, a woman of Canaan came out of the same coasts, and cried unto him, saying, Have mercy on me, O Lord, thou Son of David; my daughter is grievously vexed with a devil. But he answered her not a word. And his disciples came and besought him, saying, Send her away; for she crieth after us. But he answered and said, I am not sent but unto the lost sheep of the house of Israel. Then came she and worshipped him, saying, Lord, help me. But he answered and said, It is not meet to take the children's bread, and to cast it to dogs. And she said, Truth, Lord: yet the dogs eat of the crumbs which fall from their masters' table. Then Jesus answered and said unto her, O woman, great is thy faith: be it unto thee even as thou wilt. And her daughter was made whole from that very hour. (Matt. 15:21–28)

And from thence he arose, and went into the borders of Tyre and Sidon, and entered into an house, and would have no man know it: but he could not be hid. For a certain woman, whose young daughter had an unclean spirit, heard of him, and came and fell at his feet: the woman was a Greek, a Syrophenician by nation; and she besought him that he would cast forth the devil out of her daughter. But Jesus said unto her, Let the children first be filled: for it is not meet to take the children's bread, and to cast it unto the dogs. And she answered and said unto him, Yes, Lord: yet the dogs under the table eat of the children's crumbs. And he said unto her, For this saying go thy way; the devil is gone out of thy daughter. And when she was come to her house, she found the devil gone out, and her daughter laid upon the bed. (Mark 7:24–30)

The passages just quoted from Matthew and Mark present for me one of the most puzzling incidents in all the New Testament. The woman's obvious need and maternal heart are impossible to miss. But Jesus' response to her urgent appeal seems uncharacteristically hardhearted. Perhaps, therefore, God has some special learning hidden away, lessons requiring extra-diligent digging.

First, the location of the incident is interesting. Rather than being in the interior of the land where He mostly ministered, Jesus was near the sea: Tyre and Sidon were on the Mediterranean coast.

As in the majority of recorded incidents, we're given no name or life specifics. However, rather than being a Jew, as in earlier instances of Jesus' meeting with women, she was a Canaanite, or Syrophenician—a Gentile. Too, she was a mother. But her maternal state was marred by a horrifying fact: her young daughter was beset with an evil spirit. In those two basics the woman's self and her situation begin to come into focus.

The area God promised to His people, Israel, when they came out of captivity in Egypt was known as Canaan. Canaanites were the original inhabitants of the land, and they were idolatrous, sin-ridden people. Jehovah empowered the Israelites to conquer or destroy city after city, tribe after tribe, as they came into the land. The Jews despised the generations of natives remaining in the area. Like us today, God's people of that time wrongly hated sinners rather than hating only their sin. So the distraught Canaanite mother approached Jesus with a major strike against her, humanly speaking: her nationality. Jesus was, after all, the Jews' Messiah. Only later would come knowledge that He is the Savior of all mankind. There was another negative imbedded in the situation: Jesus had entered the house with the intention of backing off from the constant pressures of His ministry days. Notice that He asked for His whereabouts to be kept a secret. The Syrophenician woman's arrival and request, therefore, were impositions.

Another interesting detail is given in Matthew: the manner of the woman's appeal. The text reads that she "cried unto him." Hers was a rather unseemly manner: her loud voice broke into the quietness of the Lord's intended retreat. The irritation of her shouted appeal comes through to us in the disciples' urging Jesus to send her away. They complained, "For she crieth after us." Her crying out seems to indicate that she began from a distance, perhaps at first being blocked from getting close to Jesus—whether by the owner of the house, bystanders, or the disciples. The term the disciples used about her voice hints at an analogy Jesus Himself used later: a dog baying after its prey in the hunt.

Despite the fact that her words from the very first were clearly heard as she called out, Jesus ignored her. That cold response did not deter this heart-heavy mother. She continued to call out until, somehow, she broke through the human barrier and came close to the apparently unresponsive Man of Nazareth. At that point she gave up shouting; instead, she fell at His feet in worship.

Something in her addressing Jesus also holds meaning. She called Him "son of David"—identifying Him not just as Jewish but as the Messiah. Yet to this amazing recognition by a Gentile, too, He remained unresponsive.

Think now about the request she brought to the Lord. Many of you who are reading this book are mothers of one or more daughters, as I am. A girl child offers a special dimension of maternal delight through blood-and-gender bonding, as well as through a depth of understanding not possible in mothering a son. But because of those special factors, anything marring the relationship can be particularly painful. So it must have been in this instance: delight had turned to horror. We're not told exactly how the demonic activity in the girl affected her. But surely there had been a drastic change in personality and behavior, an ugly twisting of the child's mind that at times made her unrecognizable and frightening. The poor mother was an unwilling prisoner to her daughter's unpredictability. What an awful home atmosphere that would have produced. What a source of constant, fearful strain upon the woman. Perhaps, too, in her satanic torments the child became physically violent, battering herself or attacking others.

Awful situations like the one imagined here are not phenomena confined to early New Testament times. Many of us have friends or acquaintances whose lives as parents are wracked by children whose minds have been devastated and personalities changed by physiological malfunction, trauma, or drug damage. Heartbreak, frustration, and despair haunt the helpless parents. It was such emotional desperation that drove the Canaanite woman to approach Jesus so brashly. Her bold manner and loud voice adversely affected Jesus' disciples, and they added to the woman's difficulties by urging that she be sent away.

Jesus' first verbal response seems to echo the harshness of her shouted petition and to be rooted in her addressing Him as Jewish: "I am not sent but unto the lost sheep of the house of Israel" (Matt. 15:24*b*). Those words relegated her to the nations and peoples outside His main interest and intended ministry, seeming to bar further petitioning.

But the negative words didn't deter this burdened, determined mother. In fact, they may have increased her determination—as if she gathered her strength to push against that forbidding hand He had raised verbally.

After the insistency of her initial approach, the woman moved closer to Jesus and knelt worshipfully at His feet. Again His treatment of her needy soul was unlike the norm. Other moments of hard words coming from His mouth were understandable—for example, when He condemned the money-grubbing temple currency changers or when He tongue-lashed the scribes and Pharisees whose religiosity masked their own inner wickedness and led others astray. But in this instance it was a worshipful, pleading mother who heard Him say in reply to her pathetic "Lord, help me!" "It is not meet to take the children's bread, and to cast it to dogs" (15:26*b*).

No person presented to us anywhere in God's Word, from highest to lowest, from wisest to most foolish, from richest to poorest, is ever anything but wholly human. So too this Syrophenician woman. How would you or I have felt as those barbed words entered our ears? Her heart was already raw from the daily pain of witnessing and dealing with her daughter's condition: unkind words spoken by this One to Whom she was appealing had to have been emotionally crushing. How tremendously I admire her at that point. She didn't let emotional hurt derail her determination. In spite of incredible heart wounding, she joined mental discipline to maternal resolve and forged ahead. Notice how she took the cruelest of the words just spoken and made them— though rough and difficult—a steppingstone for her desperate climb to help for her beloved daughter: "Yes, Lord: yet the dogs under the table eat of the children's crumbs."

As your imagination brings the scene into life, color, and movement, don't those words strike you with amazement? She didn't argue against the stated focus of Christ's ministry. She didn't shrink at the demeaning term used to describe her unfa-vored state. By repeating the term *dog*, which He Himself used, she accepted and acknowledged her unworthiness. She humbly recognized that any help He might deign to extend would be undeserved graciousness. At that point Jesus revealed Himself once again as the tender, needs-meeting Shepherd.

Mark's passage uses an interesting phrase. Jesus said to the woman, "For this saying" (7:29*b*). Because she had accepted and expressed her unworthiness yet begged for crumbs she knew would suffice, her petition was granted. And Matthew quotes a wonderful extra: "O woman, great is thy faith" (15:28*b*).

This Canaanite woman indeed demonstrated persevering faith. That faith was richly rewarded. Jesus commended her self-effacing, earnest, upward-looking heart, and He spoke healing for her daughter. There was no dramatic incantation or pro-nouncement. Quietly, Jesus said to the woman that her faith was rewarded and her daughter freed. "Be it unto thee even as thou wilt" (Matt. 15:28*b*). "The devil is gone out of thy daughter" (Mark 7:29*b*).

The quality of the Canaanite's faith again comes through to us: the woman didn't prolong her stay. She didn't ask for some sign that healing had occurred. She went home, and there she found the joyous answer to her plea. Her daughter was no longer wildly raging but lying quietly on her bed, resting in the peace of demons departed.

$\mathcal{M}$EETING HIM WITH HER

What are some messages for us via the Syrophenician woman? Certainly there's a reminder of how important it is that I as a mother take my children's problems to the Lord. That sounds almost silly in its simplicity. However, I believe Christian parents more often neglect than activate this basic. In the first place, we too wait for a crisis before we actively represent our children before the Lord. Just as a demon had invaded this woman's daughter seeking to destroy her, Satan daily tries to destroy our children—twisting them personally, harming the family group, and damaging the testimony of Christ. Were we to plead for them daily from the moment of conception, they would be buffered from the Devil's attacks and the crises surely would be smaller and fewer. As our children grow and we hold them tightly, we too often look to ourselves or to other flesh-coated sources for the meeting of their needs.

We take it upon ourselves

~ to protect them (usually overprotect)

~ to rescue them (usually unwisely)

~ to change them (usually for our pleasing)

~ to undo their mistakes (instead of letting them learn that choices have consequences)

~ to direct them (usually into the path of our preference)

Of course all that humanity-dependent effort comes to naught. It also, in a great many cases, worsens the situation and wastes the child.

I also receive from the Syrophenician encouragement to bring my children's needs to Christ with the kind of strong determination that is willing to cry out to Him. Others may look askance at us for that intensity, as the disciples did upon her. But the bystanders' lack of understanding should not deter us. I wonder how many times prayers for our children are unanswered because we lack both diligence and strength of belief as we pray. At the same time, this desperate mother did not make demands of Jesus. She presented her problem and she pled for His help. A true believer must never badger or "command" the God of glory.

Next, the Canaanite reminds me of the importance of humility as we petition for our children's needs. Just as she accepted her unworthiness, so too should you and I. We are wholly unworthy even of coming into God's presence, let alone having Him hear and help us. All our access, all our acceptance by Him, all His response to our pleas have nothing to do with our deserving; they are entirely bound up in Christ's mercy and grace. What a constant cause for humility as we come into the presence of God in prayer! Yet I find so often in my prayers and in the prayers of those I hear around me a spirit that says in effect, "Well, here I am, God. I'm really doing pretty well on my own, but there's this thing I'd like from You, and after all You owe me this . . ."

A third lesson I see when looking at the woman in this incident is encouragement to prevail in prayer. If the distraught mother had given up in the face of apparent blockades, her daughter would have remained a victim of the demons. There are three points at which, like the Canaanite mother, I need to persevere.

First, when God is silent. There are times when my soul senses no response and I can find no applicable passage in Scripture. Second, when people around me misunderstand or criticize or gossip. And, finally, when the Word itself reminds me that in my human frame I'm unworthy of God's undertaking. In each of those instances, I must persevere in prayer, kneeling before my sovereign Lord on the cushion of Hebrews 4:16—"Let us therefore come boldly unto the throne of grace, that we may obtain mercy, and find grace to help in time of need."

DEDICATED PARENTING MUST BE TIGHTLY YOKED WITH SEEKING GOD'S WORKING IN THOSE THINGS BEYOND OUR REACH.

The glimpse God has allowed us of the Syrophenician "dog" indeed shows us much. As we leave her, may we do so instructed from the spirit expressed in Psalm 2:11: "Serve the Lord with fear, and rejoice with trembling."

Recognizing the need to pray for our children is a generalized response to the Canaanite woman's story. Before we leave her, let's probe for more specific applications. The first would be to acknowledge a child's condition. The mother in the story did not deny her daughter was wretched. She didn't try to prettify her situation. Nor did she hold back because of her own maternal embarrassment as she presented the girl's horrendous state. We mothers prefer to think of an offspring as being pretty fine at every point. And woe betide anyone who points out flaws or opposes his or her direction and desires! That attitude is foolish, destructive mothering. Every child is a sinner.

Second, when we agree with Scripture that our child is sin-marred and sin-prone, we are to undertake for him or her as faithfully and effectively as possible. God demands much of parents: we're to "bend the plant" toward His light and away from darkness—

> And thou shalt love the Lord thy God with all thine heart, and with all thy soul, and with all thy might. And these words, which I command thee this day, shall be in thine heart: and thou shalt teach them diligently unto thy children, and shalt talk of them when thou sittest in thine house, and when thou walkest by the way, and when thou liest down, and when thou risest up. (Deut. 6: 5–7)

But dedicated parenting must be tightly yoked with seeking God's working in those things beyond our reach. Ultimately, the real essence of our son or daughter is in that "unreachable" category and must be daily brought before the Lord. God has a design and a purpose for that individual, and it's He Who has the right and power to ply the right tools.

Chapter 10

THE WOMAN TAKEN
IN ADULTERY

Jesus had been apart from the throng, spending time alone with the Father on the Mount of Olives. Then, John tells us,

Early in the morning he came again into the temple, and all
the people came unto him; and he sat down, and taught them.
And the scribes and Pharisees brought unto him a woman
taken in adultery; and when they had set her in the midst, they
say unto him, Master, this woman was taken in adultery, in
the very act. Now Moses in the law commanded us, that such
should be stoned: but what sayest thou? This they said, tempt-
ing him, that they might have to accuse him. But Jesus stooped
down, and with his finger wrote on the ground, as though he
heard them not. So when they continued asking him, he lifted
up himself and said unto them, He that is without sin among
you, let him first cast a stone at her. And again he stooped
down, and wrote on the ground. And they which heard it,
being convicted by their own conscience, went out one by one,
beginning at the eldest, even unto the last: and Jesus was left
alone, and the woman standing in the midst. When Jesus had
lifted up himself, and saw none but the woman, he said unto

her, Woman, where are those thine accusers? hath no man condemned thee? She said, No man, Lord. And Jesus said unto her, Neither do I condemn thee: go, and sin no more."

I think it's interesting that only John records this temple incident—John, the one who seemed more in tune with Jesus' compassionate heart than the other disciples. The story is often taken as a text or used as an illustration within a broader outline for Sunday school lessons and sermons. What I want us to do, however, is to come into the incident as individual women looking at this individual woman in her meeting with Jesus.

The woman had been caught in the very act of sexual immorality—adultery. Does that make you feel squeamish as we approach her, as if some bits of moral dirt may cling to us by associating with her? I hope not. That reaction indicates self-righteousness—looking down our supposedly superior spiritual nose at someone we consider a guttersnipe. Such a judgmental, drawing-skirts-aside response puts us right there among the scribes and Pharisees. Rather, we must—however uncomfortably—acknowledge that she is not a sinful freak to be condemned out of hand; she's a flesh-and-blood woman. As such, she's not a bit different from any one of us, except that she did what any one of us is capable of doing. Therefore, let's come into the picture as God presents it and stand beside this nameless one with hearts open to learn.

So—she's a woman taken in adultery. Was she a prostitute? We're not told so; nor are the terms used in the narrative particularly indicative of her being a "strange woman"—in which case her sin would more likely have been called "fornication." Therefore, she seems to have been an ordinary woman who had become sexually involved with a married man—perhaps she was married as well. The term *adultery* as used in the Bible usually indicates one or both of the participants were married.

How did the woman get involved in adultery? That's not important or God would have told us. Whatever her background, personality, or life circumstances, however, it comes down to this: she yielded to temptation, choosing to satisfy lustful thoughts, physical urges, and emotional attraction. Those three deadly gateways into sexual sin can face any of us. Our Christianity, our church membership or position, our age, our social standing, our marital status—none of those things guarantee that we will not commit sin of whatever sort. The capacity for sin and the tendency to commit it pervade the being of each of us. God in His wisdom, love, and grace made us capable of choice—and throughout our lives we exercise that gift. Sadly, even after salvation our flesh continues to lean away from God rather than toward Him.

The accusers who dragged the woman to Jesus that day were the upper crust of Judaism. Not men of the street or those untaught by Scripture. Instead, their lives were dedicated to the intricate interpretations of the Scripture scrolls and to the religious traditions of their forefathers. They had become spiritual policemen, not only rigidly conformed to their own overly precise rules but also calling others to task for real or supposed infractions. They considered themselves, in effect, greatly superior to the woman against whom they brought the charges.

Have you ever wondered how and why those religious fellows laid hands upon the adulteress in the first place? How did they discover and identify her?

Had they known of the immoral relationship and ignored or tacitly condoned it until it could become useful to them? How had they caught her "in the very act"? Might it have been a set-up?

Why did they neglect to bring the man with whom she was involved? After all, the law demanded that both the man and the woman involved in adultery be stoned. Why did they thus twist the law they supposedly understood and upheld? Did they, as men, allow the adulterous man an excusing leniency they denied the woman? Did they, in masculine superiority, conveniently assume that the man had been lured into the relationship by the woman?

Did cowardice figure into the situation—constraint against dealing harshly and publicly with a man but no compunction against overpowering and condemning a mere woman?

Even to be seen with such a woman publicly as they brought her through the streets must have plagued the self-consciously pious Pharisees and their cohorts. But the animosity they felt toward Jesus was so intense, their desire to discredit Him so rabid, that they dirtied their hands with the openly sinful woman.

So there she was—brought into the temple, that edifice so honored by the Jews as their God-given place of worship. How tiny and helpless she must have felt in that enormous building. Her accusers shoved or pulled her along through the crowd gathered there to hear Jesus as He sat teaching them. Imagine the disturbance it would have caused. The woman's heart would have been icy with terror. She must have shriveled as she experienced the scorn and hatred of those surging around and staring at her. We don't know how long she had lived in the adulterous relationship; but for whatever length of time, to whatever degree her illicit situation had been known, she would have been despised by law-abiding people around her. Now she knew the absolute depth of fearful shame: both secular scorn and spiritual ostracism swirled around her, and the law demanded that she die by stoning.

Brought face to face with Jesus that day was a woman who represents the ultimate distortion of what woman was created to be. She had chosen to defy the law of God, to degrade her nature, to shatter God's prescribed, precious, pure monogamous intention. Her choice brought her to a terrifying crisis of mind, heart, and body. Between her and Jesus lay an immeasurable spiritual chasm: she was the grubbily soiled daughter of Eve; He was the sinless Son of God. Her life was that of darkness; He was the Light of life. She stood helpless and hopeless, facing deserved punishment by death; He sat the God of all power, the embodiment of eternal hope, and the One Who had come as substitute for her condemnation.

The scribes and Pharisees had created what they thought would be an effective trap for the Nazarene. Would he set aside the law of God? If He did so, He would be discredited in the eyes of the people—a dearly held hope of the "official" religious leaders. If He agreed with the law's punishment demand, His reputation for grace would be damaged, and they would enjoy demonstrating their purported righteousness as they killed the woman by stoning. They focused keenly upon Jesus, awaiting His response with smirking self-satisfaction.

But Pharisees, scribes, the watching crowd, His disciples, and the woman herself waited in vain for Jesus to speak. An ordinary human being faced with such a moment would have stammered, squirmed, and searched for words, but He did not have to speak. His silence must have been highly disconcerting. Silence is awkward even in a typical social setting. This was much more than a typical social occasion; rather, emotion and suspense would have made the air fairly crackle. But the Nazarene did not speak. He did not move, except to bend over and use his finger to write in the dirt. The silence held . . . and held. Fidgeting began in those around Him. The observers were puzzled, and they began to grow impatient. Surely this One Who a short time before had been expounding the Scriptures should speak, either to confirm that the adulteress was to be killed or to extend some sort of special exemption. The accusers hoped His lack of response to be a sign that they were successful, and soon they would hear from his lips something to destroy His reputation. So they jumped into the silence and repeated their queries—each one louder and more demanding than the one before. At last Jesus looked up from the dust and looked quietly around at those who were baiting Him. The words He spoke held nothing they had expected or hoped for. He didn't take up the woman's cause. He didn't dispute about the law. He returned the responsibility of judgment, the decision to punish the adulteress, to those men who had brought her: "He that is without sin among you, let him first cast a stone at her" (8:7).

Then He bent again to his dust-writing.

What did Jesus write as He moved His finger through the dust? Scripture is silent. Nevertheless, the scribes and Pharisees deciphered their own individual sinfulness, written with the inescapable finger of God upon their consciences. Any of a multitude of sins could have risen to the eyes of various ones that day, but I wonder somehow if perhaps conviction gripped each one in connection with this particular sin and from this specific moment—

~ each one's seeking out the woman purposefully from a hitherto unchallenged illicit relationship

~ each one's bypassing the guilt of the man with whom she was involved

~ each one's laying hands upon her and experiencing the power of her sensuality

~ each one's recognizing her beauty and physical attraction

~ each one's regretting the lack of that erotic fire in his own wife

~ each one's fantasizing

Mightn't it be possible that not one of those men could disassociate himself from the very lustfulness for which they sought Jesus' condemnation of her? Whatever it was that arose in their individual consciences, it caused conviction powerful enough that all of them had to leave the scene. The oldest men moved away first. Despite whatever years of private study and public recognition they had known, those oldsters were perhaps shocked by the exposure of their ongoing fleshly vulnerability. Before long every one of the accusers, right down to the youngest, deserted the scene.

Wiping His finger free of dust, Jesus confronted the woman—a trembling bit of human dust. In the moments just past, her heart had made an incredible journey. Clearly seeing into her repentant soul, He pronounced His forgiveness and sent her into a new, cleansed life.

As in New Testament times, so too now, we think of adultery in a woman as representing the dregs of female sinfulness. On the surface of things that is true. But the incident we've just explored should remind us, as it did the haughty religionists, that no human being has the right to condemn another. The owner of a pointing finger is just as guilty as the one accused. We need to recognize that God does not use the kind of measurements you and I do: Scripture makes clear that sins of the spirit are as heinous in His eyes as are sins of the flesh. The religionists that day in the temple were as guilty as the adulteress. They condemned her for lust of the flesh while demonstrating their own pride of life and likely experiencing lust of the eyes.

At last her devious, hypocritical accusers were gone, and the woman was left alone, standing before Jesus. Just as He had known the hearts of the scribes and Pharisees, so He knew her heart. While Jesus' silence had held and while first her accusers' voices trailed away and then they themselves faded from the scene, she had moved from extreme fear for her life to repentance for her sin. Thus, Jesus told her she was free from His condemnation. And that freedom was to be demonstrated by an entirely new kind of life: "Go, and sin no more" (8:11).

Meeting Him with Her

The "lynch mob" scene with the adulteress holds a great deal for us if we're open to its lessons. The learning comes both from the accusers and the accused.

First, what can those angry religionists teach us? Because they were steeped in the traditions of their forbears, because they fanatically dotted every "i" and crossed every "t" of religious observance, they considered themselves righteous—and so, similarly, may we. The externals can become so important to us and require such diligent maintenance that our heart connection to God thins to a mere filament. Overage in nonessentials diverts attention from everything of true importance. Romans 4:4–5 strips away such self-deception and self-satisfaction:

> Now to him that worketh is the reward not reckoned of grace, but of debt. But to him that worketh not, but believeth on him that justifieth the ungodly, his faith is counted for righteousness.

We must maintain that strategic distinction between futility and faith. Bloated self-evaluation automatically becomes others-condemnation. Personal exaltation of externals will have us judging others on the basis of externals. Jesus commanded against that in John 7:24—"Judge not according to the appearance, but judge righteous judgment."

Nor will genuine, humble faith delight in proclaiming the sins of others. Unfortunately, there is both private gloating over and public castigation of others' failures—either supposed or real—abundantly evident among us today. Just log on to some "Christian" blog. If it were measurable, self-righteous hot air would blow out the top of the temperature gauge. It was just such incendiary judgmental attitudes operating that day in Jerusalem's temple.

COMPASSION SEEMS TO ARRIVE ONLY TARDILY IN MOST OF US.

And where was compassion for the sinner among those accusers? Obviously, it was absent. Yet again, we should be slow to cast shame upon them. Compassion seems to arrive only tardily in most of us. In response to an openly sinful person, one of several words other than *compassion* would more accurately describe our reaction:

~ disgust

~ fear

~ scorn

~ horror

~ revulsion

~ condemnation

But what of heartache for her imprisonment in sin? Why no yearning for her spiritual rescue? Where is our awareness that there, apart from God's amazing, undeserved grace, go we? How utterly unlike Jesus Christ we so often are—and how frequently we resemble the rabid scribes and Pharisees.

My husband's grandfather used an old-fashioned term for a sinful woman. It picturesquely and powerfully stated truth—but compassionately. She was said to be "a soiled dove of the underworld."

Are we like the woman's accusers in another way, as well, setting ourselves up as the standard of right? There are several areas in which such self-assigned policing takes place among us in the twenty-first century:

~ dress

~ makeup

~ church attendance

~ ministry involvement

General guiding determinations can and should be set by corporate bodies—for example, a church, Christian school, or mission board. And the biblical principle of yielding to authority certainly applies to members of those groups. But matters get entirely out of kilter when individuals consider themselves the standard of biblical correctness and criticize, condemn, or ostracize anyone who doesn't come to heel. Such a holier-than-thou spirit not only fosters divisiveness but also turns unsaved people away from Jesus Christ.

Do we, like the Pharisees and scribes, misuse Scripture by applying or not applying it according to those who are involved? Is a lie labeled sin in someone else's child but considered a cute, creative remark in ours? Do we proclaim horror long and loud against a church member convicted of embezzlement while we cheat on our income tax return? Do we express disgust while inwardly enjoying rehashing details of a sexual affair involving some ministry figure? Do we tell others the latest details come to light in a person's moral failure?

Most pertinent and personal from the story of the adulteress should be our renewed rejoicing that we, like she, have undeservedly experienced the compassion of Jesus Christ rather than the condemnation earned by our sin. How constant and enormous should be our joy in the Lord's daily mercies that defy the protests by our wretched accuser, Satan.

Chapter 11

MARY OF BETHANY

The sisters living in Bethany, Martha and Mary, have been the focus of so much study, so many sermons and Sunday school lessons, that they seem nearly as overexposed as Jesus' mother, Mary. But each time my Bible reading brings me to them, they bless and instruct me. In writing of them, I neither intend nor expect to uncover anything new. I simply want us to look together at the convicting Scripture portraits of these two women. Although they're always mentioned together, we'll separate them for the sake of individualization.

It's easy to gather from reading the New Testament that Mary was a common name for girls and women. In fact, Scripture frequently adds descriptive words or phrases to distinguish the multiple Marys. We continue to do so today: we almost always refer to this particular Mary as "Mary of Bethany."

Bethany, designated as being a village or town, lay about two miles from Jerusalem. These, then, were small-town rather than big-city sisters, simple rather than sophisticated. The Bible tells us nothing of how or when Jesus became acquainted with them and

their brother, Lazarus. The text infers, though, that the relationship had been established rather early in Jesus' ministry, creating
familiarity and warmth in the friendship.

How old was Mary? We don't know; all we gather is that she
was Martha's younger sister. Since they lived together in Martha's
house, they must have been mature single women.

Here, then is a point worth considering: their singleness. Mary
and her older sister, unmarried women, figure quite prominently
in Jesus' earthly life and were the focus of His loving attention.
In turn, they believed in Him, loved Him, and ministered to
Him. Their marital state did not at all deplete their special, close
relationship to the Christ or make them second-class Christian
servants. The poet Christina Rossetti (1830–94) from personal
experience enlightens those who look askance upon singleness as
being somewhat deficient:

> She whose heart is virginal abides aloft and aloof in spirit. . . .
> Her spiritual eyes behold the King in His beauty; wherefore
> she forgets, by comparison her own people and her father's
> house. Her Maker is her Husband, endowing her with a name
> better than of sons and daughters. . . . She loves Him with all
> her heart and soul and mind and strength; she is jealous that
> she cannot love Him more; her desire to love Him outruns her
> possibility, yet by outrunning enlarges it. She contemplates
> Him, and abhors herself in dust and ashes.

That's an important reminder for our times, when some seg-
ments of our Christian community consider single women inferior
to married women in terms of potential and worth. That attitude
certainly isn't Christlike. We see Christ's special appreciation demonstrated in His relationship with Martha and Mary.

Whereas the Bible records most of the women meeting Jesus
only in one outstanding incident, we're allowed to see Mary three

times, each appearance showing her at Jesus' feet. To me, that speaks the central sermon of Mary's person and pathway: she wholeheartedly, worshipfully adored the Lord.

Let's look first at the occasion when Jesus was visiting in the sisters' home.

> Now it came to pass, as they went, that he entered into a certain village: and a certain woman named Martha received him into her house. And she had a sister called Mary, which also sat at Jesus' feet, and heard his word. But Martha was cumbered about much serving, and came to him, and said, Lord, dost thou not care that my sister hath left me to serve alone? bid her therefore that she help me. And Jesus answered and said unto her, Martha, Martha, thou art careful and troubled about many things: but one thing is needful: and Mary hath chosen that good part, which shall not be taken away from her. (Luke 10:38–42)

The position Mary chose, at Jesus' feet, indicates her purpose to glean what she could as He talked; thus she "heard his word." Her posture and proximity identify her as an eager student of His teaching. She chose spiritual activity over physical activity. She listened in a quiet, concentrated way—not satisfied just to catch snatches of conversation while coming and going.

Martha saw her younger sister's physical inactivity as thoughtless and lazy. In exasperated self-pity she pointed out the unfairness of Mary's part in the business of serving. In tattletale fashion she asked Jesus to get Mary moving. But Jesus took the contrast she'd complained of and used it to illustrate comparative values. He acknowledged Martha's involvement in many things, but neither their number nor their accomplishment compared in importance to the single undertaking Mary had chosen.

Our second glimpse of Mary comes when crisis had struck the home. We find the story in John 11.

Now a certain man was sick, named Lazarus, of Bethany, the town of Mary and her sister Martha. . . . Therefore his sisters sent unto him, saying, Lord, behold, he whom thou lovest is sick. When Jesus heard that, he said, This sickness is not unto death, but for the glory of God, that the Son of God might be glorified thereby. Now Jesus loved Martha, and her sister, and Lazarus. When he had heard therefore that he was sick, he abode two days still in the same place where he was. . . . Then when Jesus came, he found that [Lazarus] had lain in the grave four days already. . . . Martha, as soon as she heard that Jesus was coming, went and met him: but Mary sat still in the house. Then said Martha unto Jesus, Lord, if thou hadst been here, my brother had not died. But I know, that even now, whatsoever thou wilt ask of God, God will give it thee. Jesus saith unto her, Thy brother shall rise again. . . . She went her way, and called Mary her sister secretly, saying, The Master is come, and calleth for thee. As soon as she heard that, she arose quickly, and came unto him. . . . She fell down at his feet, saying unto him, Lord, if thou hadst been here, my brother had not died. When Jesus therefore saw her weeping, and the Jews also weeping which came with her, he groaned in the spirit, and was troubled, and said, Where have ye laid him? They said unto him, Lord, come and see. Jesus wept. Then said the Jews, Behold how he loved him! And some of them said, Could not this man, which opened the eyes of the blind, have caused that even this man should not have died? Jesus therefore again groaning in himself cometh to the grave. It was a cave, and a stone lay upon it. Jesus said, Take ye away the stone. . . . He cried with a loud voice, Lazarus, come forth. And he that was dead came forth, bound hand and foot with graveclothes: and his face was bound about with a napkin. Jesus saith unto them,

Loose him, and let him go. Then many of the Jews which came to Mary, and had seen the things which Jesus did, believed on him. But some of them went their ways to the Pharisees, and told them what things Jesus had done.

Martha and Mary recognized the serious nature of Lazarus's illness and sent their appeal to Jesus. In view of His loving friendship with the family, surely the healer would come to free Lazarus from his sickness.

Jesus received the message in Bethabara, about twenty miles from Bethany; yet He delayed. His response to the message was "This sickness is not unto death, but for the glory of God, that the Son of God might be glorified thereby" (11:4).

The text doesn't make clear whether that was simply a statement or if those words were given to the messenger who had been sent to fetch Him. Whatever the case, Jesus waited two days before going to Bethany. How puzzled and hurt Martha and Mary must have been when Lazarus died and they had to see him buried! When Jesus did—finally—go to Bethany, Lazarus had lain in his tomb four days. Jews did not embalm: the day of death was also the day of burial. Therefore, by the time Jesus arrived Lazarus's body would have begun to decompose.

News of Jesus' approach reached the sisters. Martha took action; Mary continued sitting quietly in the house. Why didn't she, like her sister, dash off to meet Him? In the first place, dashing was not characteristic of her personality and temperament. But why Mary's noted quietness in that particular circumstance? Perhaps there was a negative factor at work: disappointment in Jesus' failure to come could have shaken her belief. Her "sitting still in the house" might have reflected the internal calm of faith. Her quietness might have been that of calling to mind everything she had known of the Master in the past—His character observed and

His words heard. Perhaps it indicated disciplined patience, waiting until His greater wisdom brought Him to the house.

Apparently Mary was sitting somewhat apart from those who'd come to mourn with the sisters, so Martha was able to speak privately to her, relaying Jesus' summons. Only then, when Martha brought word that Jesus wanted to see her did Mary become physically active. She went to Jesus instantly and quickly. Seeing her leave the house so abruptly, the ritual mourners thought she was going to Lazarus's tomb to weep. When Mary reached the spot where Jesus had halted outside the village, she fell at His feet. Then came the only words recorded from her lips. She stated exactly what Martha had said to Him: "Lord, if thou hadst been here, my brother had not died" (11:32*b*).

By those identical opening statements, were the sisters, in their limited understanding, referring to Jesus' message that Lazarus's illness was not fatal? Was it their hearts' expression of disappointment and sorrow? Or did it state their faith in Jesus' power? Perhaps it was all three rolled into one. There can be multiple intentions in any words we speak. The Bible doesn't comment about their motivation. Unmistakably within the statement of each, however, is Mary's pronouncement of personal faith.

Whatever the main intention behind the words, Mary spoke them from her characteristic place at Jesus' feet. Think for a moment about where she knelt that particular day. There was no rug—or even flooring—under her knees, only rough roadside earth. Mary's loving, worshipful heart didn't consider dust or weeds or stones. And don't her words ring differently from Martha's despite the fact that they were technically identical? The distinction lies, I think, in the fact that Martha spoke them while she was standing, Mary while kneeling.

The final recorded scene involving Mary and Jesus came just six days before Passover—the highlight spiritual celebration in the Jewish calendar. In all the years since Moses, God's people Israel had celebrated His sparing them when He sent death to every other household in Egypt. The Passover lamb's death was central to that celebration, memorializing the blood-marked doorways that had insured their salvation. Matthew, Mark, and John recorded the Bethany incident occurring so shortly before the Passover in which Jesus, the Lamb of God, was to die. His blood would, once for all, provide eternal salvation for any who would put their trust in Him. Scripture allows us to witness the profound moment of Mary's final kneeling.

> Now when Jesus was in Bethany, in the house of Simon the leper, there came unto him a woman having an alabaster box of very precious ointment, and poured it on his head, as he sat at meat. But when his disciples saw it, they had indignation, saying, To what purpose is this waste? For this ointment might have been sold for much, and given to the poor. When Jesus understood it, he said unto them, Why trouble ye the woman? for she hath wrought a good work upon me. For ye have the poor always with you; but me ye have not always. For in that she hath poured this ointment on my body, she did it for my burial. Verily I say unto you, Wheresoever this gospel shall be preached in the whole world, there shall also this, that this woman hath done, be told for a memorial of her. (Matt. 26:6–13)

> And being in Bethany in the house of Simon the leper, as he sat at meat, there came a woman having an alabaster box of ointment of spikenard very precious; and she brake the box, and poured it on his head. And there were some that had indignation within themselves, and said, Why was this waste

of the ointment made? For it might have been sold for more than three hundred pence, and have been given to the poor. And they murmured against her. And Jesus said, Let her alone; why trouble ye her? she hath wrought a good work on me. For ye have the poor with you always, and whensoever ye will ye may do them good: but me ye have not always. She hath done what she could: she is come aforehand to anoint my body to the burying. Verily I say unto you, Wheresoever this gospel shall be preached throughout the whole world, this also that she hath done shall be spoken of for a memorial of her. (Mark 14:3–9)

Then Jesus six days before the Passover came to Bethany, where Lazarus was which had been dead, whom he raised from the dead. There they made him a supper; and Martha served: but Lazarus was one of them that sat at the table with him. Then took Mary a pound of ointment of spikenard, very costly, and anointed the feet of Jesus, and wiped his feet with her hair: and the house was filled with the odour of the ointment. Then saith one of his disciples, Judas Iscariot, Simon's son, which should betray him, Why was not this ointment sold for three hundred pence, and given to the poor? This he said, not that he cared for the poor; but because he was a thief, and had the bag, and bare what was put therein. Then said Jesus, Let her alone: against the day of my burying hath she kept this. For the poor always ye have with you; but me ye have not always. (John 12:1–8)

Using John's account as our basic text, let's examine the incident's richness in order to honor Mary's heart and to edify ours.

"Then," the beginning word, refers, of course, to time and place. But what were they? Jesus was with disciples and friends in the house of Simon, a leper whom He'd healed earlier at a brief stop on the way to Jerusalem—and Calvary. Thus, we see a very public moment for a very private expression. Mary was not in the comfortable familiarity of her own home, and she was greatly outnumbered by the men present. Earlier incidents reveal her as a woman who was quiet and retiring rather than forward in any way. The public setting, then, didn't lend itself naturally to her action. Nevertheless, there in another's house, at a supper attended by a group of men, Mary responded to her heart and performed an act of personal worship.

Having established time and place, we now move on to the next noteworthy phrase: "a pound." Here we're told the quantity involved in her act. We can immediately sense her generosity. Mary didn't dole out an ounce or two with a mind to what would be sufficient; she gave lavishly. Surely far less than a pound would have provided enough to perform the anointing—which was more an act of hospitality and honor than of cleansing.

My husband and I had the privilege a number of years ago to visit the little emirate of Bahrain as guests of the American ambassador. Those days were some of the most interesting we have ever known. Besides attending official receptions, we were also kindly invited for evening meals in private homes. As we would enter a house, the host and hostess would greet us warmly with words and smiles. Then they would indicate a servant who stood nearby with a tray of very expensive perfumes and colognes. As guests, we would choose a scent to spray or dab on our wrists and neck. The Middle Eastern custom in Bahrain greatly helped me conceptualize Mary's ointment incident. Our "ointment" was distributed in tiny, tiny quantities from containers holding only a few ounces; Mary's pound of ointment was indeed highly generous.

The Bible identifies Mary's offering as "ointment of spikenard." That's a nice, rather melodic combination of words, but what does it mean? "Ointment" is a positive word, and today we generally think of it as a healing agent to relieve pain or to prevent infection. It connotes both purity and purifying. Obviously, then, Mary presented a generous portion of something good that day.

There is a further dimension of meaning in Mary's ointment. The descriptive words "of spikenard" infer that the balm was pleasantly aromatic, or perfumed. This information moves us to think beyond the gift's quantity to its quality. There are at least two aspects of the ointment's quality to consider. The first is that of emotional value. Such a perfumed substance would have personal meaning to Mary as a woman. We feminine beings take pleasure in perfumes and colognes. Solomon well stated such pleasure in Proverbs 27:9a: "Ointment and perfume rejoice the heart."

I grew up with a living illustration of womanly love for scents: my mother. Although she was financially unable to own anything but cheap cologne, any visit to a department store or drugstore would find her happily indulging her olfactory sense. As soon as we entered the door, she would head for the fragrance counter. Once there she'd generously apply the samples—not just one or several, but all of them—and then happily walk on through the store amid a multilayered cloud of mingling and competing fragrances.

No doubt there was some other suitable and effective possession Mary could have chosen to use in her act of anointing. Instead she used something that she valued personally.

There is a second aspect in terms of value seen in the term "ointment of spikenard." Twenty-first century Americans have no understanding of the ingredient—yet it's important to the pictured incident. Spikenard was a plant prized for its aromatic quality, valued not only for the pleasant aroma itself but also because of its rarity: the plant grew exclusively in certain areas of India. So Mary's gift was not equivalent to a drugstore or discount store purchase. Instead, it was a specialty import. We can have some idea of imported fragrances today in terms of rarity and cost. But when we consider what manufacture and importation involved in the first century B.C., our understanding of value expands.

As if God wanted to underline the enormousness of Mary's heart gift that day, He moved John to include the term "very costly." Or, as Matthew and Mark put it, "very precious." Each of the writers—men—recording the incident recognized the financial significance involved. Why? Evidently, containers of ointment like Mary gave were typical of womanly treasures in that era. The men's practical minds translated such emotion-laden riches into monetary value. No wonder—because study reveals that purchasing ointment of spikenard in that one-pound quantity would have cost nearly a full year's wages! Why would an ordinary woman like Mary have such a valuable possession? We don't know. But because its nature and value were readily recognized by the three Gospel writers, I wonder if such special items might in some instances have been the crown jewel in a woman's hope chest.

Further insight comes to us from Matthew and Mark. They note how the ointment was packaged: in an alabaster box. So, apart from the expensive ointment, even the container itself was valuable. The container also introduces another facet to this diamond-like demonstration of a woman's love for Jesus Christ. The spikenard-scented ointment, because of its precious, rare nature, was hermetically sealed into the beautiful container. That means Mary had to break the seal—or perhaps even the container itself—in order to anoint Jesus' head and feet. She held nothing back, saved none of the treasured possession for herself. Her gift was not just a gift; it was a sacrifice.

Now we arrive at the manner of Mary's bestowal. We find that she applied the fragrant ointment both to Jesus' head and to His feet. To anoint His head, she may have been standing or stooping, and the action would have been relatively brief and ceremonial. Anointing His feet, however, demanded the major portion of her time and attention. To perform that service as it's described, she would have had to kneel. Mary lived in a day when, rather than sitting in chairs like we do, people reclined around a low table.

Look closely at Mary kneeling there in humble service to the One she loved so greatly. Listen. Do you hear anything? No. She knelt in the silence of worship. Why was Mary silent? Because she had full heart knowledge of Him before Whom she knelt! He was no ordinary man; He was the invisible God clothed in human flesh. He was, in Isaiah's words, Wonderful, Counselor, the mighty God, the Everlasting Father, the Prince of Peace. So, soundlessly, Mary went about her act of devotion, anointing the feet of her Lord with her sacrificial gift.

Did others in the room continue their conversations, unheeding? Did they suddenly cut short their talk, silenced and made uneasy by Mary's act? Or did their captured attention immediately produce strong and critical comments like those recorded a bit later? We don't know—and Mary didn't care.

Having drenched Jesus' feet with the sweet-smelling ointment, Mary proceeded to wipe His feet with her hair. Several things speak to me from that action. First, she would have had to unbind or uncover her hair; the common practice at the time had only "strange women" in public with uncovered, free-flowing hair. She thus defied contemporary practice. Second, Mary had to bend lower still in order to dry Jesus' feet. That made a demand upon her physically. Think—she was already kneeling on a hard floor; now she must bow her back in order to use her hair as a towel. Moreover, there is another physical sacrifice demanded by her act: oily hair. The word *ointment* infers at least some oil content in the mixture, and probably a great deal of it. Oily hair is generally something we women do our best to avoid. But Mary sacrificed personal preference for profound expression of love.

Another phrase reaches out from the passage, and it clamps my heart in an iron grip: "the feet of Jesus." When Mary knelt before Him that long-ago moment, His feet were whole and strong from miles of walking and healthily browned from hours in the Middle Eastern sun. When I kneel today at His feet, they bear the awful wounds of Calvary's nails—nails driven through His flesh and bone because of my sin. Jesus did not pull away from Mary's touch. Nor does He pull away from my touch. Jesus— eternal, immutable, all-powerful God come to earth in flesh to save us. O Love divine, boundless and eternal in its forgiveness and longsuffering!

The anointing scene there in the home of Simon closed with an interesting phrase: "And the house was filled with the odour of the ointment" (John 12:3). I can never read those words without being captivated by the beautiful, fragrant witness of Mary's devotion to Christ. The lovely aroma of her God-loving heart wafted out to everyone present that evening.

You would think that as the ointment's fragrance permeated the house it would sweeten the atmosphere. Not so. Instead, there was sharp criticism and rebuke for her having wasted financial resources. "And there were some that had indignation within themselves, and said, Why was this waste of the ointment made? For it might have been sold for more than three hundred pence, and have been given to the poor. And they murmured against her" (Mark 14:4–5).

Notice that Mary made no response to the disciples' sniping, but Jesus spoke up in her defense. "Then said Jesus, Let her alone: against the day of my burying hath she kept this" (John 12:7).

Did Mary herself know the expanded meaning of her act? I believe she did, based upon the fact that Scripture indicates she was absent from among the other women who gathered after the crucifixion to anoint His body for the tomb. If she did thus anticipate Jesus' death, Mary had a breadth and depth of spiritual perception considerably greater than that of the disciples.

What just one woman did in a matter of moments in love for her Savior was stamped as timelessly significant by Jesus' further words: "Verily I say unto you, Wheresoever this gospel shall be preached in the whole world, there shall also this, that this woman hath done, be told for a memorial of her" (Matt. 26:13).

The verses following Jesus' commendation of Mary reveal yet another interesting aspect or result of those moments:

> Then one of the twelve, called Judas Iscariot, went unto the chief priests, And said unto them, What will ye give me, and I will deliver him unto you? And they covenanted with him for thirty pieces of silver. And from that time he sought opportunity to betray him. (26:14–16)

"Then" Judas went to betray Christ! The darkness of Judas's character is starkly silhouetted against the light of Mary's shining so brightly in the earlier moments.

> Then saith one of his disciples, Judas Iscariot, Simon's son, which should betray him, Why was not this ointment sold for three hundred pence, and given to the poor? This he said, not that he cared for the poor; but because he was a thief, and had the bag, and bare what was put therein. (John 12:4–6)

It seems that Mary's worshipful love worked like a knife, shredding Judas's already frayed tether of restraint.

That a woman's worship could ignite a man's horrific fury should not seem strange. Scripture repeatedly states that those who are wicked hate the righteous. Too, the bloody trail of martyrdom throughout history continues to proclaim spiritual antagonism to this very day.

But come back now to that One Who is central in the incident, and as He was shown to be central in Mary's life. Because of a woman's worshipful act, Jesus on that evening in Simon's house experienced one final, serene moment of love before He went on to face the hurricane of hatred that lay ahead.

Meeting Him with Her

There really is no part of Mary's character, bearing, and life that doesn't wring my heart with conviction. Yet her exemplary self doesn't stand as an unreachable, unrealistic goal for personal attainment because I have been privileged to know modern Marys. In fact, even as I write today at my computer, tears come to my eyes thinking of one such lovely lady of the Lord. God took her home this past week. She and her husband were classmates with us in college. In those youthful days and through all the years since, Billie consistently demonstrated Mary-like sweetness. It was as if her every cell were permeated with the aroma of her worshipful heart—and we who knew her were blessed and inspired.

So, then, knowing such Mary-ness to be attainable, let's personally apply what we've seen at Bethany.

Certainly the woman's quiet heart is a characteristic to be emulated. Whatever was going on around her, wherever she was, Mary exuded an air of settledness. I think we can trace that spiritual solidity back to the few words she's recorded to have spoken: "Lord, if thou hadst been here, my brother had not died" (John 11:32*b*).

Did you notice that Jesus, in responding to her, did not query her further as He had Martha? There was no need to do so. Mary's faith in Him was full and firm. She had proven that fact repeatedly in a number of ways. Day by day you and I can make the same choices.

~ She chose to be at Jesus' feet.

~ She opted against talking in favor of listening to Him.

~ She chose contemplation of His teaching.

~ She exercised herself unto godliness.

~ She didn't just take in; she grew spiritually.

~ She looked toward that which is eternal.

Mary beautifully demonstrates the spirit I should have as I come to the Lord in my devotional time. Listening in vain for her voice, a dart of painful conviction strikes me. My "busies" cling too tightly as I open the Word, keeping my soul from the silence of openness to Him. Then when I close my Bible and move on to pray, I'm often talking before my knees even hit the floor. God tells me to be still in order to know Him. And the better I know Him, the more I can pray with quiet faith that He hears and will answer.

We twenty-first-century believers have such a sketchy, incomplete concept of the great I AM that we bounce, babble, and burble in His presence most unfittingly. We thus dishonor that unique, eternal, all-powerful One, Who reminds us, "I, even I, am the Lord; and beside me there is no saviour" (Isa. 43:11).

Beyond the loveliness of her overall character, the incident in which Mary anointed Jesus' feet presents multiple lessons for personal learning. Even that little time-and-place-setting word *then* grabs and shakes me. Mary demonstrated her heart for Christ oblivious of the publicity of the moment. Yet when an invitation is given after a powerful Scripture sermon or lesson, don't I tend to let the public setting derail my need to respond openly? After all, who wants to walk an aisle and let everyone know you have a spiritual need!

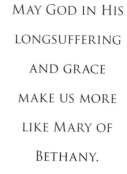

MAY GOD IN HIS LONGSUFFERING AND GRACE MAKE US MORE LIKE MARY OF BETHANY.

Do the words *generous* or *sacrifice* really apply to my life for Christ? In terms of ministry appeals, offering plates, missionary projects, believers in devastating circumstances, do I give with a responsive heart and open hand? When the need demands surrendering something that means a great deal to me personally—like Mary's ointment of spikenard—will I make the sacrifice?

Even the little, little thought about oily hair pokes an accusing finger: don't I sometimes turn away from an opportunity to serve the Lord and His people because it would demand something of me physically? For instance, preparing a meal for a sick neighbor or friend, helping to create a special ladies' event, volunteering for a full-Saturday workday at the church?

In leaving Mary there in Simon's house, the question comes, what is the testimonial odor of my life? Think for a moment what various negative essences may waft forth daily.

Maybe it's the reek of onion as we allow bitterness and complaint to taint our spirit. Or is it garlic those around us detect—the garlic of criticism and harshness? Perhaps it's only the "mild" odor of pride's cabbage. What an all-pervading, persistent reek that makes! In thinking through those and the many other convicting points that come to mind, I'm moved to pray that the outstanding odor of my life may not even be bacon: necessary and legitimate life activities.

May God in His longsuffering and grace make us born-again women more and more like Mary of Bethany: worshipfully serving Him and blessing others with the lovely aroma of quiet, faithful devotion.

Chapter 12
MARTHA OF BETHANY

I f you're a woman who, like me, knows the enjoyment of having a sister, you've no doubt often felt or expressed amazement at how different you are. Although born of the same parents and growing up in the same home, individualities are unmistakable. That was certainly true with Mary and Martha.

Studying Mary, we found quietness of spirit, body, and tongue. Coming now to Martha, we find much the opposite. That in no way indicates that she was inferior or unworthy. Instead, it might serve to remind us of God's infinite variety in creation. Not one of His created human beings is without purpose and worth. Satan wants to limit, blight, and destroy us individually; our Creator desires to expand, bless, and use us. Martha, as well as Mary, provides valuable teaching for us women who follow her.

Perhaps some of Martha's distinguishing characteristics were attributable to birth order: she appears to have been not only the older of the sisters but also perhaps the firstborn, older even than Lazarus, since their home in Bethany was designated as "Martha's house." Because of that indication, too, it seems the three siblings were unmarried. Because of her position in terms of age, Martha exercised some degree of authority and decision making. Innate leadership is often characteristic of firstborn children.

In writing the above paragraph, I had to smile, remembering the days of our children's growing up. Because our firstborn, a son, survived only two hours beyond his birth, our daughter, Roxane, captured the vacated leadership spot. And she planted the flag firmly. From earliest days with her younger brothers, she was decisive and outspoken. Her claim to supremacy was not always accepted or appreciated by Bob and Stephen—but it was seldom relinquished. So our home saw *firstborn* or *elder*, as terms, take on life. Having watched "the leadership gene" so clearly active in our daughter's childhood, we have delighted in its replacement by submission to her husband's leadership in marriage.

Now back to Martha. Sometimes sermons and Bible lessons tend to second-rate her out of hand while elevating her sister, Mary, to near-angelic status. Scripture doesn't do that: it portrays both women honestly—but both are seen as women of character, distinct personalities, and active love for Jesus Christ.

So, first of all, Martha is worthy of admiration for her ministry of hospitality. Remember, she was single—a fact that in many cases today serves as an excuse against a food-and-fellowship, bed-and-board ministry—or any other. Martha seems to have provided hospitality for Jesus and His disciples on a regular basis. We sense from the text that as a result of those frequent visits Jesus enjoyed a particularly close friendship with the family members there in Bethany. As owner of the house, it was Martha who decided when, how, and how frequently to take in Jesus and His disciples. Such occasions meant much more than just a simple dessert and coffee: in hosting the group there would have been at least thirteen guests coming for a full meal! Houses of that day were not large;

therefore, the meals for Jesus' group would have meant considerable crowding. Obviously, then, Martha was a practical and capable person who could handle logistic challenges.

She also comes across as a hard worker. Think what her hostessing demanded in that day when just keeping a house clean would have been a major project:

~ Every piece of clothing and household linens would have been hand-woven and constructed.

~ Every food item was grown or made from scratch.

~ There was no running water.

~ Refrigeration did not exist.

~ Cooking was a backbreaking job done without an electric or gas stove, oven, or microwave, but using a fireplace and clay oven.

Despite the difficulties and the countless hours the work demanded, Martha chose to minister to Jesus' group. Why? Because she had a heart for people's needs; she wanted to be of service. We women know that hospitality is much more than a matter of our hands. It springs from the heart: a heart that wants to encourage others and is willing to sacrifice effort and time for that purpose.

Opening her home and providing food for Jesus and His followers was neither a tea party with small, fancy finger food nor a buffet from which guests served themselves. Rather, it demanded food served in sufficient substance and abundance to satisfy the hunger of men—men who, in most instances, had been walking for miles. Imagine their appetites and consumption! Yes, Martha definitely deserves admiration and appreciation for the succor she provided so often. Her hospitable spirit and hard-working hands made a genuine, important contribution to Jesus' ministry.

Having established our basic, positive approach to Martha, let's go on to study the specific instances where she appears in the Gospels.

> Now it came to pass, as they went, that he entered into a certain village: and a certain woman named Martha received him into her house. And she had a sister called Mary, which also sat at Jesus' feet, and heard his word. But Martha was cumbered about much serving, and came to him, and said, Lord, dost thou not care that my sister hath left me to serve alone? bid her therefore that she help me. And Jesus answered and said unto her, Martha, Martha, thou are careful and troubled about many things: but one thing is needful: and Mary hath chosen that good part, which shall not be taken away from her. (Luke 10:38–42)

"Martha received him into her house." Good for her! If she'd not extended that invitation, not taken on that extra responsibility and labor, where would Jesus and His disciples have found the refreshment they needed that evening? Would it have been yet another day in which, moving through the countryside, they grew so hungry that they plucked corn and ate it raw? Mary sat at Jesus' feet, drinking in His every word. Meanwhile, Martha scuttled—cooking, carrying food, refilling empty plates and cups, working, working, working. It's easy to see in this that Martha was a physically active woman. Sitting was foreign to her. I know many women like that. Because they are bundles of perpetual motion, they're able to accomplish far more than we women who are less actively inclined. That was Martha; and in watching her scuttle there, perhaps the Lord would nudge you and me to be more like her in terms of physical activity for the sake of His name and His people.

So far, so good in our Martha inspection; and remember, we don't know how many meals she had served the group before this particular incident. Now, though, we hit a snag. On this occasion the hostess was busily serving her guests—but her manner of serving was askew. She was "cumbered" about it; in other words, her scuttling was done with grim determination, tense concentration, and a joyless spirit. The logistics and practicalities involved in feeding all those people had become a burden.

It's difficult for me to be too hard on Martha because I identify with her problem through experience. However eagerly an invitation may have been given, whatever expectations of fellowship opportunity are involved, however happily the menu was chosen, whatever fun there was in setting the table and preparing the food, there often comes a moment of "cumbering." Mine usually hits when I'm working at the kitchen sink between the main course and dessert. I'm there in the kitchen working fast and furiously, rinsing plates and flatware, analyzing what's needed to get dessert plated and into the dining room. Those moments, of course, are while everyone else is sitting around the table enjoying relaxed conversation. Yes, I can identify with Martha!

Martha didn't keep her encumbered spirit to herself—she voiced her irritation about Mary's noninvolvement and complained about her own overwork. Notice where she directed her complaint—not to Mary the offending sister but to Jesus! And listen to what she said: in effect, she accused Him of being unfeeling and unfair. She did so while addressing Him as "Lord!" I find the reality of that contradiction jolting. Martha certainly had nerve, didn't she? Or perhaps it was just that she'd built up such a head of steam, getting more and more angry over her "suffering," that her mouth outran her mind. Does that ever happen to you? It certainly does to me! However, even in that moment of Martha's

complaint to the Lord, I sense a positive for my heart: Martha had
such a close relationship to Jesus Christ that she could be direct
and honest in her speech with Him. Our communications person-
to-person differ greatly according to the relationships involved.
The less we know a person, the less comfortable we are, and
the less open in expressing thoughts and emotions. We establish
interpersonal boundaries, protecting ourselves and limiting the
other person's access to our mind and heart. Closeness encourages
freedom of expression. That distinction operates spiritually as well.
A slight, distanced acquaintance with God makes prayer language
stiff and restrained. But time spent with Him and knowledge of
Him does away with chilly formality. It nurtures intimacy and
honesty. Martha could have approached Jesus with a simpering,
phony-sweet presentation of her case. But she wasn't the type to do
so, and the quality of their relationship didn't warrant it.

Now witness Jesus' response. He didn't rebuke Martha for her
approach to Him. In fact, His words and the spirit they inferred
seem to confirm the special nature of their relationship: "Martha,
Martha" (10:41*b*). I hear in His repetition of her name fondness
and warmth. You and I use such name-doublings in speaking to a
child, a relative, or a very close friend.

Notice the focus of Jesus' reply: He didn't point to her busyness or to her irritation with Mary but to the spirit of her labors.
His concern came through in the words *careful* and *troubled*.
Despite the fact that Martha was rendering a necessary, valuable
service, she had become so tensely caught up in what she was
doing that she'd caused a deficit in her being.

This is a point at which many of us Christian women can
profitably consider our own lives. Even those who are officially
"retired" bemoan the constant busyness of life. It's almost as if our
earthen globe has increased its axial speed of whirl, and we who

live on it must race to accommodate the acceleration. In doing so, our sense of value can become badly skewed, and the "inner man" shrivels in the heat of hurry. Many times in my life it has been as if God through His blessed Word remonstrated, "Beneth, Beneth . . . " Having captured Martha's attention and stilled her hustling, Jesus then targeted her overlooked, core necessity—not just in terms of the moment but rather for all of godly living: "But one thing is needful" (10:42*a*).

So much in our daily lives and in our service for the Lord is necessary only in the loosest sense. Yet how consistently our heart, mind, and hands focus upon those very things! Jesus says to each of us, "Only one thing is needful." The single essential for you and me is a vibrant personal relationship with Jesus Christ—and His abiding spirit of peace. Martha had momentarily sacrificed those as she buzzed about her duties. The importance of our relationship with the Savior may be firmly established in our minds, but keeping it an operative reality is difficult. Moment by moment we must struggle against triviality's tyranny.

There was an object lesson at the moment, and Jesus used it: Martha's own sister. He didn't go into an extended treatise on discernment or prioritizing. He simply directed Martha's attention to Mary. Both physically and attitudinally, Martha's younger sister demonstrated the more mature spirituality.

Martha's discernment of relative values had been distorted, yet we shouldn't shame or condemn her. After all, even the most glorious, expansive landscape disappears from view if we hold a small object close to our eyes. That was Martha's problem. Momentary work had obscured eternal worth: "Mary hath chosen that good part" (10:42*b*).

The second important truth imbedded in Jesus' commendation of Mary is in the verb *hath chosen*. Distractions and minimally important pursuits are not forced upon us—we choose them. Moment by moment throughout every day we make decisions about where our attention and activities will be invested. That's not a comfortable reminder because it destroys our excuses and silences our protest of overwhelming circumstances. Jesus was making that point in what He said to Martha. Consider the Lord's final phrase: "Which shall not be taken away from her" (10:42c).

The guests would leave after the evening meal, the house grow silent, the food and conversation become only a memory, and Martha would go to bed to rest her weary body. Clearly, she was concentrating on that which was transient and depleting whereas Mary was pursuing the permanent and enhancing.

I think it's important to clarify what Jesus did not say or infer that evening.

~ He didn't tell Martha not to work.

~ He didn't say that sitting is always to supersede serving.

~ He didn't say Martha's choice was useless.

If we mistakenly read those things into the incident, we can come away misdirected. First, we'll feel discouraged and rebuked in doing the numberless tasks that fall to a woman each day. Or we'll use the incident as permission for laziness that masquerades as spirituality.

Often when I read this passage, my mental VCR replays an experience I had near our family room door one morning. I was hurrying to leave the house for work. As I came out the door, a small flower plot caught my attention: two creatures were moving there. One was a bee, the other a butterfly. I paused briefly to watch them, and the sight lifted my heart. It stayed with me as I went on to work, expanding from simple observation to worthwhile meditation. Both the butterfly and the bee are God's creations, and they serve a like purpose: pollination. But how differently they fulfill their task! The bee zips along with its wings moving so rapidly they create a buzzing sound, and the wings themselves become invisible. The butterfly, too, has wings—but how differently they move! They provide their owner with transportation that is not only effective but also fascinatingly beautiful. In the little garden plot that morning, which little flyer drew my attention in the more positive sense, and to which was I drawn personally? The butterfly, of course: the bee's impressive busyness served as a warning to avoid it! There are Martha and Mary: we need to recognize the positive accomplishment of beelike Martha but seek at the same time to reflect the lovelier, graceful spirit of Mary.

Now we move on to the later incident in which Scripture lets us see Martha—the illness and death of Lazarus, her brother.

> Now a certain man was sick, named Lazarus of Bethany, the town of Mary and her sister Martha. (It was that Mary which anointed the Lord with ointment, and wiped his feet with her hair, whose brother Lazarus was sick.) Therefore his sisters sent unto him, saying, Lord, behold, he whom thou lovest is sick. When Jesus heard that, he said, This sickness is not unto death, but for the glory of God, that the Son of God might be glorified thereby. Now Jesus loved Martha, and her sister, and Lazarus. When he had heard therefore that he was sick, he abode two days still in the same place where he was. (John 11:1–6)

Notice, first, that both sisters were involved in sending the appeal to Jesus: they were actively united in their concern for Lazarus and in the attempt to get Jesus to come heal him. Second, look again at the sentence describing Jesus' relationship with the family: "Now Jesus loved Martha, and her sister, and Lazarus" (11:5).

My heart always wants to cheer as I read that because Martha's name is listed first. In other words, Martha is not considered the "also-ran" of the sisters by Spirit-breathed Scripture.

The tone of the sisters' appeal to Jesus is also interesting: "He whom thou lovest is sick" (11:3*b*).

Rather than a lot of persuasive words or an urgent description of Lazarus's health crisis, the women joined in a simple reference to the strong emotional ties between Jesus and their little family.

But there were two days of delay before Jesus went to their village home. The Bible doesn't describe or comment upon how Mary and Martha occupied that tense, disappointing, and ultimately grieving time. Much can be imagined, however, because of what's seen in the women before and after. Mary's typically quieter choices would have contrasted with Martha's active, tense ones. In the pressure of their brother's illness and death, distinction of temperaments even may have been a mutual irritation. It's not unusual for flash points to occur among family members at times of stress because of contrasting individualities. Martha and Mary certainly display those differences clearly as the Scripture narrative takes up again.

> Then when Jesus came, he found that he had lain in the grave four days already . . . and many of the Jews came to Martha and Mary, to comfort them concerning their brother. Then Martha, as soon as she heard that Jesus was coming, went and met him: but Mary sat still in the house. Then said Martha unto Jesus, Lord, if thou hadst been here, my brother had not died. But I know, that even now, whatsoever thou wilt ask of God, God will give it thee. Jesus saith unto her, Thy brother shall rise again. Martha saith unto him, I know that he shall rise again in the resurrection at the last day. Jesus said unto her, I am the resurrection, and the life: he that believeth in me, though he

were dead, yet shall he live: and whosoever liveth and believeth in me shall never die. Believest thou this? She saith unto him, Yea, Lord: I believe that thou art the Christ, the Son of God, which should come into the world. And when she had so said, she went her way, and called Mary her sister secretly, saying, The Master is come, and calleth for thee. . . . Now Jesus was not yet come into the town, but was in that place where Martha had met him. . . . When Jesus therefore saw [Mary] weeping, and the Jews also weeping which came with her, he groaned in the spirit, and was troubled. And said, Where have ye laid him? They said unto him, Lord, come and see. Jesus wept. Then said the Jews, Behold how he loved him! And some of them said, Could not this man, which opened the eyes of the blind, have caused that even this man should not have died? Jesus therefore again groaning in himself cometh to the grave. It was a cave, and a stone lay upon it. Jesus said, Take ye away the stone. Martha, the sister of him that was dead, saith unto him, Lord, by this time he stinketh: for he hath been dead four days. Jesus saith unto her, Said I not unto thee, that, if thou wouldest believe, thou shouldest see the glory of God? Then they took away the stone from the place where the dead was laid. And Jesus lifted up his eyes, and said, Father, I thank thee that thou hast heard me. . . . And when he thus had spoken, he cried with a loud voice, Lazarus, come forth. And he that was dead came forth, bound hand and foot with graveclothes: and his face was bound about with a napkin. Jesus saith unto them, Loose him, and let him go. Then many of the Jews which came to Mary, and had seen the things which Jesus did, believed on him. But some of them went their ways to the Pharisees, and told them what things Jesus had done. (John 11:17–46)

When at last Jesus responded to the sisters' appeal for help and came to Bethany, Martha's home was again filled—this time with those who had come to mourn Lazarus's death. Apparently he had died while the messenger was on his way to Jesus. We're told specifically that Lazarus had lain in his grave four days. The four-day length of time certified for all Jewish observers that his death was real. In turn, they also certified the reality of his miraculous return to life.

The text indicates that the sisters' response to their brother's loss again demonstrated their contrasting personal patterns. Martha was "buzzing" among the friends and neighbors who'd come to sympathize; Mary had chosen to be removed from them. The elder sister was probably, again, busy about the household duties that accrued when numbers of people visited. And, true to form, when she heard Jesus was near, she charged out of the house to waylay Him. And, as earlier, she was direct in what she said to Him. Notice her certainty that if Jesus had come in time, her brother would not have died. There is beauty of soul and strength of faith evident in her words as she proclaimed, "Even now" (11:22b).

All hope for Lazarus in the human sense was gone—but Martha's faith wasn't bound by human experience and possibility. She went on to verbalize the extent of her belief: "Whatsoever thou wilt ask of God, God will give it thee" (11:22c).

In some ways Martha was ahead of most of Jesus' disciples in terms of belief and commitment. That is clear in her further declaration after Jesus posed the direct question concerning His being life itself. "She saith unto him, Yea, Lord: I believe that thou art the Christ, the Son of God, which should come into the world" (11:27).

Most of His disciples still struggled with wholehearted belief at that point. No wonder Jesus loved the little family of Bethany! They refreshed Him not only physically through gracious hospitality but also spiritually through solid faith.

Following that conversation, Martha returned to the house and summoned her sister. Then Martha's sense of proprietary oversight surfaced again as the little group stood before Lazarus's grave. Jesus asked that the grave be opened. Horrified, she offered a verbal protest: "Lord, by this time he stinketh: for he hath been dead four days" (11:39*b*).

Martha's response was understandable. Imagine her emotional hurt at the thought of seeing her beloved brother's body rotting in its shroud! Imagine the unpleasantness for those standing near when the inevitable reek of physical disintegration would emanate from the tomb. Martha was a thoughtful, practical woman as well as a spiritually advanced one. That is an admirable combination of characteristics.

Jesus' response to Martha's protest didn't in the least rebuke the practical concern she had expressed. Instead, He took her back to the earlier moment in which she'd proclaimed her faith. "Said I not unto thee, that if thou wouldest believe, thou shouldest see the glory of God?" (11:40).

Martha's faith would be fulfilled momentarily. Jesus' general statement would become specific reality, and what her heart had affirmed, her eyes would confirm. I love the fact that the sisters were there at the grave together to share the unimaginable experience of their brother's return from the dead. Those two dear women, so different and yet so alike, had their simple ministry to Jesus more than rewarded by that moment. When Lazarus stepped—living—from his grave, Mary and Martha witnessed a faith-sealing glimpse of Christ's eternal, limitless power.

The raising of Lazarus was a capstone for the believing family members, but it ignited the final, determined religious enmity against Him as well. One whose power was demonstrated so inarguably had to be stopped before He could destroy the religionists' power over the people. From the moment Lazarus came from his tomb, Jesus' path more distinctly led toward His own. However, just as Lazarus shed his grave clothes, so too would the Savior shed His—in promise that we shall do likewise.

---

*M*EETING HIM WITH HER

Probably most of us identify more readily with Martha than with Mary because Mary seems almost otherworldly in her quietness, sweetness, and all-encompassing devotion to Jesus Christ. So, then, perhaps Martha's lessons for us can be more readily perceived and received.

Certainly each of us can examine the competing areas of spiritual and practical involvement in our lives, see Martha's weaker choice, and determine to strengthen our own focus upon the eternal so we spend more time with and for Him. The need for such strengthening is constant and lifelong. Our flesh is "too much with us" from morning to night every day of our lives here on earth.

Too, in our demanded, practical pursuits we constantly need to monitor the spirit we bring to each task. My "monitor" finds me woefully needy so many times. The conflict between maximal to-dos and minimal hours tempts toward strained nerves and burdened brain. What a huge service Martha can render there! First, she can serve as the conduit for Jesus' analysis of a cumbered spirit; and, second, she can reflect the warmth of encouragement as we're reminded that "Jesus loved Martha . . . " So, too, does He love and patiently deal with each of us modern Marthas—whether that identification be applicable to a lifetime temperament or to a momentary embroilment.

Martha's honest approaches to Jesus also challenge my heart. Since He of course knows the contents of my inner self before they ever find expression in words, my verbal conversations with God really should reflect Martha's in that they are honest and informal while simultaneously always honoring Him as Lord. "Wherefore we receiving a kingdom which cannot be moved, let us have grace, whereby we may serve God acceptably with reverence and godly fear" (Heb. 12:28). As Martha grew in friendship with Him through real-time visiting and service, so should I.

BOTH SISTERS LOVED AND WERE LOVED BY JESUS CHRIST, THEIR CREATOR AND SAVIOR.

I love the fact that it was Martha, that ever-busy, God-chided woman who was privileged to speak one of the simplest, most direct and beautiful declarations of faith in and identity of Jesus as the Messiah, our Savior. It has occurred to me in writing this that as Mary so wonderfully expressed her love and faith while kneeling to anoint Jesus' feet, Martha did just as wonderfully as she stood with Him at her brother's grave. Each woman gave Him honor and proclaimed her faith according to her distinctive personality. If Martha had tried to re-form herself into Mary's sweetness, she would have been phony. And Mary transformed into Martha's bustle and brashness is unthinkable. Both sisters loved and were loved by Jesus Christ, their Creator and Savior. God doesn't ask us to get out of our skin; He wants us to love and serve Him in our unique personal structure—which He, after all, designed and then formed in our mother's womb. The sisters of Bethany both beautifully illustrate that fact.

Chapter 13

THE BOWED-TOGETHER WOMAN

Coming to this woman who met and was changed by Jesus, we immediately get a mental picture of her distorted physical carriage. Visualizing her unnatural doubled-over posture has an impact upon our approach to studying her. It arouses our sympathy as we imagine what it would mean to be so handicapped.

> And, behold, there was a woman which had a spirit of infirmity eighteen years, and was bowed together, and could in no wise lift up herself. And when Jesus saw her, he called her to him, and said unto her, Woman, thou art loosed from thine infirmity. And he laid his hands on her: and immediately she was made straight, and glorified God. (Luke 13:11–13)

Since her physical self is the first thing told us about her, let's consider its likely life-complicating effects. The description, "a spirit of infirmity," first, reminds me of Scripture's unfailingly straightforward, honest presentations. How unlike our day! Having wandered far from God's Word in every aspect of living, our civilization delights in euphemisms and politically correct terminology—as, for an example germane to this woman's circumstances—terming a handicap a "physical challenge." Our ever-weaker culture attempts in this and other ways to whitewash unpleasant truth. Not so the Bible! This woman was not well. If the condition of her internal organs had not actually contributed to her distorted posture, they certainly would have been adversely affected by it through those eighteen years. God designed the human body to function maximally in an upright position. Her bent-double physique not only made it impossible for her to enjoy normal human life but seems to have weakened her entire system. While the world around her bustled on its way, she was slowed and hindered by her body's betrayal.

Her malady had not been active just for days, or weeks, or months, but for years. That twisted body had imprisoned her for almost two decades. When illness or disablement strikes, timing and time become newly important. We're not told at what age this woman's infirmity began: but whenever its onset it would have meant limitations imposed upon her at an inconvenient time because physical maladies and convenience are always enemies, not friends. And what was the nature of the onset? We're left to wonder. Was it sudden, as perhaps resulting from an injury to her spine? Or maybe it was a creeping thing, beginning with a vague ache or weakness, then worsening day by frightening day.

And how achingly long she'd had to endure those and whatever other difficulties were forced upon her by her condition! I recall the longest period of physical disability I've personally experienced: a time of injury from a ski fall. I spent several months pretty much out of commission while my spine healed. Those days and nights crawled while I endured all the life complications created by being set aside. What if those months had stretched into years—eighteen years? Throughout my downtime there were indications of improvement—glimmers of hope that the debilitation was lessening and would eventually end. This dear woman had none of that.

What changes might she have experienced in terms of her womanhood: changes made against her will, then continuing or worsening through those eighteen years. Perhaps her condition prevented her planned marriage, as the man to whom she was betrothed backed out of his—or his parents'—commitment. Or it certainly would have marred a marital relationship in terms of physical intimacy with her husband. The deformity might have caused her to be barren. If conception took place, she surely would have experienced extreme difficulty in pregnancy and delivery.

Even thinking of her life in its most ordinary moments makes us realize the constancy of pressures imposed by her deformity. Her doubled-over form would have made even routine housework tough—in an era when it was already hard because of crude living conditions. Imagine the extraordinary difficulties involved in her cooking, cleaning, and shopping.

Her physical distortion would have had consequences outside the walls of her home as well as within them. In general social terms, how many times had her strange shape been disconcerting to adults or frightened children or even perhaps sent dogs scurrying? Her unusual posture also very likely brought cruel jibes from unfeeling adults and poorly taught children as she made her way through the streets day by day. She might even have become a byword among local mothers as they threatened their children with similar deformity if they lied or disobeyed. Although some of her peers would have been kind and tried to be helpful, others no doubt shunned her, not knowing how to relate to her.

The specific Scripture description—"bowed together"—furthers our empathetic response. Imagine yourself literally doubled over physically. Almost certainly there would be discomfort—perhaps to an extreme degree. A body doesn't get twisted out of its normal configuration without terrific pressure of some sort. Whether the change came through a structural weakening that made it impossible to maintain normal posture or whether there was a forceful muscular or skeletal torque, pain would have been involved at some stage, if not chronically.

I doubt that such physical twisting could take place without great emotional and attitudinal challenges. In fact, I get a sense of that very thing in the phrase "spirit of infirmity." How helpless and frightened she must have felt as the condition manifested itself, as it progressed despite everything she might have tried against it and as it finally froze her into extreme crookedness of body. Because of her bent-double posture, she was unmistakably different from other women around her. Such negative distinctiveness would have been hard to bear at any age. If all or some of the deformity had marked her teen years, her agonizing awareness of freakishness would have been enormous. She doubtless struggled just as you or I would—wrestling with fear, resentment, self-pity, anger, despair, and bitterness.

Her distorted physical condition in turn distorted her view of life. Her gaze necessarily would have been earthward; to see around or in front of her would have demanded struggling with that rigid posture. The more I imagine moving with her through a typical day, the more boggling her situation appears.

However intensely she hated her condition, whatever difficulties it created for her, or how much embarrassment she suffered, the woman was absolutely helpless "and could in no wise lift up herself." Whatever exercise she may have tried in an attempt to strengthen muscles was useless, any manipulation or massage of joints without effect, and all steel-willed determination wholly frustrated. The eighteen years she had already endured signaled endless future years of ongoing physical imprisonment. How bleak! Helpless against her body's betrayal, she must also have been hopeless against her inner yearning; she could neither see nor imagine any opportunity for release, apart from eventual death.

But then she met Jesus of Nazareth.

It was then she experienced the moment that changed everything in her life—and all of herself—forever. The Scripture presentation indicates a "circumstance" of time and place. "And he was teaching in one of the synagogues on the sabbath" (Luke 13:10).

It was the Sabbath—the Jewish day of worship. The meeting took place in the synagogue—the public building in which Jews gathered each week. The setting tells us something important about this needy individual. She hadn't let her distorting physical infirmity twist her inward self: she'd not retreated into self-absorbed, self-protective isolation. She hadn't allowed her lack of understanding the "why" of her condition or the impossibility of freeing herself from it to turn her away from Jehovah in bitterness. She hadn't made the easy, face-saving choice of staying home, where she would have been protected from curious, dismissive, or repulsed stares. She had come to the synagogue to sit under the teaching of God's Word. This woman had the kind of character amid affliction that challenges each of us, regardless of our physical state.

I wonder what effort it meant for her to have been there in the synagogue that day. How much weariness or pain had she ignored as she woke and got out of bed? How much distance lay between her home and the synagogue? How many times was she jostled and hindered by the crowds as she moved through the streets? How often had some hurrying individual collided with her because her bent form was below his line of sight? How many times had a scavenging dog barked at her strangeness? How many determined strides of her own feet could she have counted because her eyes were necessarily focused downward?

We don't know the answer to any of those questions. But what a reward she received for her perseverance! "When Jesus saw her, he called her to him, and said unto her, Woman, thou art loosed from thine infirmity" (Luke 13:12).

Did Jesus see the woman as she entered the room where He was teaching, or did she catch His attention as His eyes swept over the assembled hearers in the room? I somehow feel that it was the latter: He recognized her need even as she occupied the one position in which she didn't appear strange—seated. Whether others in the audience realized her deformity or not, He did. As she responded to His calling her forward, everyone in the room recognized the extremity of her need.

Jesus spoke just seven words. They were in the form of a statement. He asked her nothing; He required nothing of her. Seven simple words stated her release from the long years' cruel binding. It seems from the Scripture that He spoke those words of her healing while she was still bent. If so, she heard the marvelous proclamation while looking not at His face but at His feet. Isn't there a special, tender dimension conveyed by that probable position? The crucial moment found her gazing at that most common, least auspicious part of the human anatomy, feet. That earthbound perspective may have increased her sense of the impossible; her comprehension must have stalled at the contrast between ordinary feet and His miraculous freeing declaration. "And he laid his hands on her: and immediately she was made straight" (13:13).

Amazed disbelief gave way at Jesus' touch, and warmth surged through her body, unlocking her joints, melting her long-frozen posture into fluid, upright stature. She was straight! In the same instant her body was freed, so was her tongue: she testified of God's grace and power. She knew beyond all doubt that the teacher's words and touch were not merely human but also divine, and she proclaimed that reality before the crowd assembled there in the synagogue: "And [she] glorified God" (13:13*b*).

In the synagogue that day this woman experienced a transformation that surpassed the merely physical. She entered the building a pathetic, anonymous cripple. But the moment she stood upright, she became something else: an irrefutable testimony for Jesus' messianic identity—and a threat to the religionists who stubbornly retained their spiritual deformities.

> And the ruler of the synagogue answered with indignation, because that Jesus had healed on the Sabbath day, and said unto the people, There are six days in which men ought to work: in them therefore come and be healed, and not on the Sabbath day. (13:14)

Imagine! To have witnessed what happened that day and yet refuse spiritual sightedness himself and try, as well, to maintain the blindness of others. Picture what "saying unto the people" probably involved: dealing with his own shock at the woman's healing, gathering support from his cronies, and frantically trying to calm the hubbub of the congregation. Then, when he could make himself heard, proclaiming in religious arrogance that Jesus had violated the Sabbath and that those with personal or loved ones' needs must not dare to do so! The spirit of the religious leader that day, as well as the numberless others he represented, comes through clearly: "with indignation." They had no sense of awe for Jesus' power or joy for her miraculous healing. Rather, they were furious because their precious traditions were being blown. Jehovah had of course established the Sabbath centuries prior in the time of Moses. But following generations had obscured its meaning and distorted its purpose by adding nitpicky regulations. So tightly bound were they that day in multiplied, contorted Sabbath rules, the religious leader rebuked the very Lord of Sabaoth! Clearly, the woman had been made straight, but those with ministry responsibility remained crooked and bent earthward.

> The Lord then answered him, and said, Thou hypocrite, doth not each one of you on the sabbath loose his ox or his ass from the stall, and lead him away to watering? And ought not this woman, being a daughter of Abraham, whom Satan hath bound, lo, these eighteen years, be loosed from this bond on the sabbath day? (13:15–16)

Jesus powerfully addressed the supposed spirituality versus the real carnality of the religionists. They lacked not only spiritual wisdom but common sense as well.

Dead religion could not prevail that day against the vibrancy of Jesus' healing power. The onlookers, seeing the crooked woman made straight, recognized and gloried in heaven's own power come down to them in the form of a man. Truth had at last re-entered their synagogue. "And when he had said these things, all his adversaries were ashamed: and all the people rejoiced for all the glorious things that were done by him" (13:17).

The testimony of the woman healed would not have been confined to the synagogue. Rather, from that day forward she would have walked it out everywhere she went: the change in her was obvious and unmistakable. No longer forced to look at the ground, she surely took immense delight in telling of that One Who had raised her to walk upright and had enabled her to look above.

*M*EETING HIM WITH HER

Perhaps no one reading this chapter personally identifies with the physical posture of the woman Jesus healed that day. As we imagine it, though, we certainly can understand the deformity's unrelenting influence. But let's go further and use her affliction as an illustrative doorway into an area where we can identify. Walking through the door will demand courageous honesty: let's contemplate our spiritual posture.

Many individuals among Jesus Christ's believers around the world in this twenty-first century are spiritually bent double. Some have maintained the strange, unhealthy posture for years. Others recognize their distortion shortly after it strikes and seek God's straightening. But no one consistently avoids twisting into such shape. Bent-over posture may overtake us in a moment, or it may come as a gradual bending away from uprightness.

Ecclesiastes 7:29 reads, "Lo, this only have I found, that God hath made man upright; but they have sought out many inventions." God created man spiritually upright ; then man's "invention" rendered him sinfully crooked. God's re-creation through the shed blood of Jesus Christ removes the permanence of sin's downward twist, yet any individual through his "invention" can resume bent-over posture.

The psalmist prayed in Psalm 19:12–13, "Who can understand his errors? cleanse thou me from secret faults. Keep back thy servant also from presumptuous sins; let them not have dominion over me: then shall I be upright, and I shall be innocent from the great transgression." In that prayer I see some important thoughts we can apply to the matter of our spiritual posture.

First, let us refer to our errors and secret faults. Because salvation does not erase our human structure, erroneous thoughts and acts mark our daily lives. In some instances, the errors even are hidden—or "secret"—from our own consciousness. The downward bent may be so slight that we're not aware of it ourselves. Hence the psalmist's prayer for the Lord's thorough cleansing. I have experienced a physical parallel to the spiritual factors being discussed here. When I was a young teenager, I unwittingly took on slump-shouldered, pot-bellied posture because I'd suddenly grown taller than all of my friends. Without realizing it, I was trying to be short. Although the adjusted posture was beyond my notice, it was evident to my older sister, Pat. In accord with her forthright, feisty personal makeup, she undertook my straightening. Her method contained absolutely nothing of subtlety. At various opportune moments when we were alone together, she would double her fist, sock me in the stomach, and say "Stand up straight!" Modeling school it was not—but the training course was highly effective. So, too, in my spiritual walk the Holy Spirit has used the Word much like that doubled fist.

David next prayed concerning "presumptuous sins." We can picture presumptuous sins as small increments of bending away from God dependency. That is, we make an assumption that He will allow, approve, or bless a choice we make or action we take. We do not seek the Lord's mind in the matter; we're simply making our own decisions, figuring He will go along with us. Anytime I do that, I'm bending away from uprightness. I'm bowing earthward. The more often I do it, the more easily I bend . . . the more easily I bend, the more normal the bent posture seems. If I get into that doubled-over posture long and often enough, it becomes characteristic. When such distorted carriage is physical, its presence is unmistakable. When it is spiritual, however, it may be hidden from others and give slight if any concern to the one it marks. But, ladies, it is a twist away from uprightness. Our view will be altered. Our walk will be hindered. Think how those realities may play out.

Just like the woman in the incident recorded for us, so too with you and me. Doubled-over posture forces our eyes toward earth. And what do we see there? Dust, rocks, and mud. And what do we miss seeing? The sky that spreads its glorious expanse overhead. When as a believer I've become twisted downward, earth's characteristics and difficulties are constantly evident to me; they sadden and discourage. Although a view of heaven is desperately needed, it's beyond my capability. How much beauty and joy I miss because of my posture!

> HOW MUCH
> BEAUTY AND JOY
> I MISS BECAUSE
> OF MY POSTURE!

We'll be slowed in progress by bent-over posture. Instead of moving forward steadily along the path of God's purpose, we'll hesitate, intimidated by things ahead and around us that can only be half-seen in our stooped state. Slowing even can be so great that we are never able to reach the goal God has set. Who has not seen such a Christian? Whether man or woman, that person who began as an individual of tremendous potential allowed circumstances or people to become twisting factors, failed to call upon the Lord for His straightening touch, walked on in that pathetic bowed-together posture, and ended earthly life with little or nothing accomplished for God.

On that Sabbath so long ago in the synagogue Jesus saw that bent-together woman and picked her out from all those around her who were upright in their posture. So, too, does He see you or me when we're spiritually distorted. He calls us to Him in order that we might have His marvelous cure. Will we respond and move toward Him? He won't force us to do so. We're free to ignore His call and to remain prisoners of our posture.

How terrible if the bent-together woman had ignored or declined Jesus' beckoning voice. How terrible if we do so, thus missing His release to uprightness with its resulting joyful freedom and expanded life service.

"[She] could in no wise lift up herself" (Luke 13:11*b*). Neither can we free ourselves from spiritual double-bend. We must have the straightening touch of Jesus Christ.

Chapter 14
THE MOTHER OF
JAMES AND JOHN

Our introduction to this woman who came to Jesus is somewhat roundabout: she's called "the mother of Zebedee's children." Two other things about her, for whatever reason, were not included here: she was a sister of Jesus' mother Mary, and her name was Salome.

> Then came to him the mother of Zebedee's children with her
> sons, worshipping him, and desiring a certain thing of him.
> And he said unto her, What wilt thou? She saith unto him,
> Grant that these my two sons may sit, the one on thy right
> hand, and the other on the left, in thy kingdom. But Jesus answered and said, Ye know not what ye ask. Are ye able to drink
> of the cup that I shall drink of, and to be baptized with the
> baptism that I am baptized with? They say unto him, We are
> able. And he saith unto them, Ye shall drink indeed of my cup,
> and be baptized with the baptism that I am baptized with: but
> to sit on my right hand, and on my left, is not mine to give, but
> it shall be given to them for whom it is prepared of my Father.
> (Matt. 20:20–23)

In some ways this Scripture scene tickles my funny bone, while in other ways it speaks a stern warning to my maternal self. James and John, sons of Zebedee, had the nickname "Sons of Thunder," yet here they were coming to Jesus with their mother to petition favored treatment! How humorous to think of those two grown men coming to Jesus figuratively holding to their mama's apron strings. Sons of Thunder indeed! The subject of their request was not just something they'd pulled out of thin air. Jesus had earlier said that His apostles would occupy twelve thrones with Him in His kingdom, which apparently wasn't enough for Zebedee's family:

> And Jesus said unto them, Verily I say unto you, That ye which have followed me, in the regeneration when the Son of man shall sit in the throne of his glory, ye also shall sit upon twelve thrones, judging the twelve tribes of Israel. (Matt. 19:28)

First in examining this incident, notice the spirit they seemed to have had as they came: "Worshipping him, and desiring a certain thing of him" (20:20). Was their worship genuine? Or was it simply a manufactured, emotional prelude to their real purpose? Were they primarily giving their hearts' adoration or grasping for their hearts' desire? Jesus saw the latter to be true. He didn't address their bent knees but their extended hands: "What wilt thou?" (20:21).

And, notice, He directed the question to Mrs. Zebedee. I wonder why. Had she hitherto demonstrated an overly forward temperament? Had she shown too-close maternal involvement with her full-grown sons? Was she known as being generally ambitious for them? Was there something in the men's behavior, speech, or appearance that signaled a mother's coaching? Was she in this moment obviously bursting to speak? Whatever the case, she was certainly quick to respond and not in the least hesitant or

humble: "Let my boys be co-rulers with You in Your kingdom."
Amazing, isn't it?

Rather than speaking further to Mrs. Zebedee, Jesus turned
to James and John, the would-be occupiers of prime spots in His
kingdom. "Are ye able to drink of the cup that I shall drink of,
and to be baptized with the baptism that I am baptized with?"
(20:22).

And whether in their own ignorant self-confidence or because
of their mama's incessant contribution to their egos, they came
back with the equivalent of "Sure thing!" Oh yes, there's thunder
in the fellows, certainly: the thunder of self-applause.

I wonder if Jesus' response, with its compassionate prophecy of
their suffering, had any reality for the men or their mother. I wonder if any of the three felt rebuked by Jesus' reminding them of
God's choice in the matter of who would sit in the places of honor
at His right and His left. We're not told. At least the three are not
recorded as saying anything more; that saves us further embarrassment for their self-promotive spirit.

The timing of this incident worsens the selfish focus that is so
evident in Zebedee's wife and sons. Jesus had just told His followers of His imminent suffering and death:

> Behold, we go up to Jerusalem: and the Son of man shall be be-
> trayed unto the chief priests and unto the scribes, and they shall
> condemn him to death, and shall deliver him to the Gentiles to
> mock, and to scourge, and to crucify him: and the third day he
> shall rise again. (Matt. 20:18–19)

Their request's coming after the foretelling of His agony
shows how scanty was the trio's attention upon Christ and how
fulsome upon themselves. "And when the ten heard it, they were
moved with indignation against the two brethren" (20:24).

The other disciples recognized the error in the threesome's unabashed appeal for special recognition. It's interesting that Jesus didn't rebuke Zebedee's family members for their effrontery. Instead, there is tenderness as He indicated their future suffering: "Ye shall drink indeed of my cup, and be baptized with the baptism that I am baptized with" (20:23*b*).

Then Jesus used the incident to teach the entire group that genuine Christianity is marked by the spirit of servanthood rather than self-advancement. It is unbelievers who are characterized by one-upmanship and domination of others:

> Ye know that the princes of the Gentiles exercise dominion over them, and they that are great exercise authority upon them. But it shall not be so among you: but whosoever will be great among you, let him be your minister; and whosoever will be chief among you, let him be your servant: even as the Son of man came not to be ministered unto, but to minister, and to give his life a ransom for many. (20:25*b*–28)

We're told nothing of Mrs. Zebedee's reaction to Jesus' gentle rebuke. But I believe we can get a clue from the fact that she was silenced by it. That's unlike her earlier verbal boldness. The difference indicates a distance she traveled mentally, emotionally, and spiritually in those moments. What had seemed reasonable became unthinkable, the heart so ambitious became ashamed, and her spiritual self was at least a bit loosened from its earthward tether.

Although Mrs. Zebedee showed appalling maternal pride and ambition in approaching Jesus, her spiritual failure of the moment is offset by a later mention found in Matthew 27:55–56 in a report of the scene at the cross:

> And many women were there beholding afar off, which followed Jesus from Galilee, ministering unto him: among which

was Mary Magdalene, and Mary the mother of James and
Joses, and the mother of Zebedee's children.

I'm especially glad that Mrs. Zebedee was among the women
witnessing Jesus' crucifixion. That says good things about her in
terms of spiritual growth and dedication. We can hope that in the
remaining days prior to Golgotha she had begun to live out Jesus'
challenge for selfless living: "Not to be ministered unto, but to
minister" (Matt. 20:28*b*).

*M*EETING HIM WITH HER

We who experience motherhood share multiple characteristics
and needs. We can see something of both universality and distinction by using the method of comparison and contrast between the
Syrophenician woman and Zebedee's wife.

Like the Syrophenician, she went to Jesus on behalf of her
children. Note, too, that she represented her children before
Christ when they were adults. Yes, she sought wrongly; but at least
she sought Him. One of the heartbreaks I experience is in seeing Christian mothers who seem to feel that when a child turns
seventeen or eighteen he or she can be left to make his or her own
choices. What a recipe for disaster. The late teens do indeed call
for modifying parental control—but every increment of loosen-
ing must be counterbalanced by tightening parental prayer. Only
God can give a young person the wisdom to make right choices
at such a strategic point in life. There is no age at which we dare
stop praying for our children. Lifelong maternal prayer-wrap

of children is strategic. We've all heard stories of instance after instance in which a mother's prayers have proven to be crucial in a child's salvation, spiritual renewal, escape from danger, and so forth.

There is an obvious difference between the manner of the two mothers shown us in Scripture—the manner of their approach to

HOW

THOROUGHLY

AND HONESTLY

DO I EXAMINE

MY PRAYER

REQUESTS FOR

MY OFFSPRING?

Jesus. The former came to Him in utmost humility, kneeling before Him. Zebedee's wife walked in with prideful presumption. What conviction that contrast brings: how can I ever come into Christ's presence unaware of His greatness and my little, undeserving self?

Further contrast comes to mind in thinking of the two mothers. The Syrophenician besought the Lord for help in her child's legitimate need; Salome asked for supply of their wants. The first sought against satanic power; the second actually reflected the Devil's prime characteristic, pride. So, then, how thoroughly and honestly do I examine my prayer requests for my offspring? Our human hearts are so unremittingly devious that we can wrongly identify our own desires as well as our children's needs.

Mrs. Zebedee's concept of her sons was high flown, to say the least. What about my opinion of my offspring? Is it realistic? Apparently Salome thought her sons were worthy of the honor she sought for them. On that point she serves as an extreme example of oversize valuation of one's progeny. The enormity of her blunder can awaken us to the same maternal tendency in ourselves.

It's important, of course, to have a constructive opinion of each child God gives us. We're to focus on his or her positives and consistently encourage toward worthy goals. But realism needs to play a strong part in parenting too. We must neither imagine nor inflate a child's abilities. Look around you: you'll see children being destroyed on the altar of parental ambition.

Spiritual balance is a major need in us Christian mothers—but it's difficult to maintain, often being swept aside by emotionalism. Spiritual balance keeps us aware that every child is born a sinner and continues through life in the flesh—whether saved or unsaved. Each not only can choose to sin, but usually will; sin is the default setting for every human being.

I would particularly warn mothers against believing your child doesn't lie. One of the strongest universal characteristics of our younger generation is lying. Ask anyone in Christian ministry who deals with youth. Children not only lie—instantly and brazenly—they also lie about lying for hours on end. Please don't automatically believe your child's version of any troublesome experience. There are always two sides to a situation, and your child's viewpoint will of course be colored by his or her self-protective hue. Satan, that liar from the beginning, is successfully passing along his lie gene to today's youth.

There may have been another factor in Salome's request of Jesus: she may have been trying to pull strings because of her family connection as Mary's sister. Pulling strings is a favorite ploy of ambitious or over-protective mothers. I've seen a number of them: asking favors on the basis of whatever reason or relationship can be dreamed up. If there were such thoughts operative in Salome, they serve as another point of distinction between her and the Syrophenician, who, rather than having connections, pled as an outsider and purely on the basis of need.

Since we know nothing of the Syrophenician mother after the one recorded incident, our closing must necessarily focus on Salome. And, indeed, her recorded meeting with Jesus makes me take a big step back so that I can really listen personally to Jesus' words that day—words about living to serve rather than be served. Evidently, Zebedee's wife stopped pursuing recognition and instead gave herself to unheralded service for the Lord Jesus—following Him to the cross. Will I do the same?

Chapter 15
WOMAN WITH TWO MITES

In the last recorded event of Jesus' public teaching, He pointed out, spoke of, and commended a woman. In the strictest sense, the Lord really didn't meet this individual. But He saw her and used her as a positive example. She became a means of spiritual teaching to those with Jesus that day in the temple, and she continues to stand as such for us today. Both Mark and Luke recorded the moment as follows:

> And Jesus sat over against the treasury, and beheld how the people cast money into the treasury: and many that were rich cast in much. And there came a certain poor widow, and she threw in two mites, which make a farthing. And he called unto him his disciples, and saith unto them, Verily I say unto you, that this poor widow hath cast more in, than all they which have cast into the treasury: for all they did cast in of their abundance; but she of her want did cast in all that she had, even all her living. (Mark 12:41–44)

> And he looked up, and saw the rich men casting their gifts into the treasury. And he saw also a certain poor widow casting in

thither two mites. And he said, Of a truth I say unto you, that this poor widow hath cast in more than they all: for all these have of their abundance cast in unto the offerings of God: but she of her penury hath cast in all the living that she had. (Luke 21:1–4)

In this incident let's first think in terms of Jesus' location. "He sat over against the treasury" (Mark 12:41). He was not active at that moment; instead, He was quietly observing people as they entered the temple to worship.

In our modern churches we accommodate the giving of tithes and offerings with collection plates or bags or with boxes located at the back of the sanctuary or in the lobby. In Jesus' day, however, the temple had thirteen trumpet-shaped chests placed around the walls in the court of the women. Jesus could have been teaching or preaching, but instead He was watching worshipers present their gifts of money.

Any onlooker probably could have discerned differences in amounts given by the rich and the poor. The text tells us that many of those who were prosperous gave generously. In terms of donated amounts, they were doing something highly significant for the maintenance of the temple building and support of its ministers and ministries. Their hands—admirably—were open. Of course not all the wealthy gave richly. Scripture records that distinction, and life illustrates the same each day and in many ways. But Jesus did not focus on the temple attendees who were materially rich. Instead, He looked at someone who could barely survive materially. He also wanted those who were with Him to see her: "He called unto him his disciples" (12:43).

We don't know why the disciples were not at Jesus' side at the moment. But He drew them in from their various places and activities, turning their attention to an individual among the throng of worshipers. "And saith unto them."

Even further, He personally affirmed the lesson's importance: "Of a truth I say unto you."

The phrases "verily" and "of a truth" appear throughout the Gospels , and they always introduce authoritative words of Jesus. They're like verbal bold lettering: "Get this." Having thus indicated the importance of what He was about to say, He stated the real value of the woman's giving: "This poor widow hath cast more in, than all they which have cast into the treasury: for all they did cast in of their abundance; but she of her want did cast in all that she had, even all her living" (Mark 12:43) and "this poor widow hath cast in more than they all: for all these have of their abundance cast in unto the offerings of God: but she of her penury hath cast in all the living that she had" (Luke 21:3–4).

Jesus was speaking to His disciples, who were themselves poor in terms of worldly goods. He succinctly put before them a living illustration of relative values.

Think of the great contrast in the amounts of money involved on that occasion. Many of those who had come to the temple from homes of sufficient or abundant supply gave large amounts. The richer giving versus the poorer impresses human judgment, and it supplied a large part of the overall collection for the day. But Jesus pointed out that in proportion the widow's gift was far greater because she gave from her poverty. Giving by the rich was easy; hers was hard.

The widow gave two mites. Although we're centuries removed from that period of history, we can perceive the coins' negligible value singly as well as their joint equivalent noted as a farthing. But Jesus wanted His disciples of that day—and of ours—to see beyond coinage to commitment. How differently we would assign spiritual worth if we looked past money to motivation, past the hand to the heart, beyond service to spirit.

A mite was a tiny copper coin: the smallest denomination then in use, and each was worth only about one eighth of a cent. The widow's coins put into the trumpet-shaped temple chests were so small they probably fell silently due to the musical clinking of large, multiple coins of gold and silver. But God heard the coins fall. He knew the commitment to Him they represented. The woman, designated by the words *poor* and *widow*, proved herself to be spiritually rich because her gift indicated wholeheartedness. We see here small coins and large commitment. What is commitment, anyway? It's giving of oneself, dedication to a cause or a person. The widow was committed to the Lord Jehovah. She was inspired by and faithful to her relationship to Him rather than intimidated by the crowds of prosperous worshipers or by the richness of their giving.

The widow's gift indicated something else also. It revealed compassion. Temple collections provided support for the priests in the form of food and clothing. The woman, being in financial straits, probably was poorly clothed and scantily nourished herself—but concern for the needs of those who served took precedence over her own needs. What a beautiful picture she gives of overlooking one's own needs in order to help others. As I contemplate that picture, I put around it the frame of Proverbs 19:17: "He that hath pity upon the poor lendeth unto the Lord; and that which he hath given will he pay him again."

I see in this woman's giving a final and basic factor of her being: character. She could have used her widowed state and her poverty as excuses for not contributing anything. Instead, she thought and acted on the basis of personal responsibility. Her life was hard, but she didn't hesitate to do a hard thing. Strong character makes accurate valuations. The widow's heart echoed the exclamation of Proverbs 16:16—"How much better is it to get wisdom than gold! and to get understanding rather to be chosen than silver."

We are told neither where the widow came from that day nor where she went when she left the temple, but she occupied her tiny slice of time there in such a way that she stands as an enduring example of genuine, generous giving from a committed heart.

*M*EETING HIM WITH HER

The poor widow follows Zebedee's wife in Scripture sequence. What contrast they represent! We're introduced to the former in her grasping, the widow in her giving.

The first impression on my heart in this temple scene is God's observant eye. The temple structure was huge, the crowd large and moving; yet Jesus focused upon a person you or I probably never would have noticed. At every stage of Christian life it is well to remember that regardless of time or setting, we are constantly observed by God. Awareness of His gaze should have multiple effects: encouragement, comfort, and restraint against sinning. "The eyes of the Lord are in every place, beholding the evil and the good" (Prov. 15:3).

Too many times we may think of God's eyes upon us only in a vague and general way. For a moment let's consider His gaze as it functioned so specifically there in the temple long ago. He was marking people as they came to worship. Surely He does so with you and me as well. Jesus pointed out the widow's giving—and what was indicated by it. Underlying her gift was the self she brought to worship.

What of the self you and I bring to worship services? Are you the same from one to another of those times? I'm not. There are occasions when I attend with joyful eagerness; others when weariness or distraction makes attendance merely a duty. In some services I'm sharply focused upon and responsive to the truth presented in music and word; but others make little or no impression upon either mind or heart. And so it goes. How arresting to be reminded by this Scripture story that the Lord Jesus—now seeing all from heaven—is watching and evaluating our every attendance. Whatever the outward, formal observance might be, the important thing is that my inner reality please Him.

Let's move beyond thoughts of general worship attendance to thoughts of giving. First, the matter of tithing: any pastor will tell you how energetically members of his church deny the necessity to tithe and rationalize giving as little as possible. While false religions, political parties, and adherents of ungodly social agendas pour money into their pet institutions and endeavors, we Christians give so sparingly that vital ministries have to close their doors; pastors, Christian school teachers, and missionaries struggle to make financial ends meet; and the blessed gospel of Jesus Christ is hobbled. Shame on us! How appropriate that we heed the Lord Jesus as He points to the widow and commends her selfless giving.

There is a further consideration in connection with the gifts we bring in times of worship: our giving is a time to think about our living. "Therefore if thou bring thy gift to the altar, and there rememberest that thy brother hath ought against thee; leave there thy gift before the altar, and go thy way; first be reconciled to thy brother, and then come and offer thy gift" (Matt. 5:23–24).

In other words, our horizontal doings reflect our vertical ones, and vice versa. The Christian life is meant to be consistent throughout. When our relationships with other people are askew, our relationship with God is damaged.

Another thought occurs to me as I stand there in the temple with the widow. She easily might have been turned aside from presenting her tiny gift by at least two things: the temple itself and the people around her. The temple structure was huge and ornate; its appearance could well have made a worshiper

THE CHRISTIAN
LIFE IS MEANT TO
BE CONSISTENT
THROUGHOUT.

think there was no need for supportive gifts. Because the other people gathered there were better able to contribute than she, the widow could have withdrawn, convinced that she had nothing to offer. I hear similar evaluations expressed today about various ministries—"It's too big to need my money" or "It has so many supporters it can do without me." Hence, an excuse against giving financial support or being an active participant. On that long-ago day, however, the widow looked beyond the physical setting and the attendees to the spiritual reality as designed by God Himself: God's work is to be supported by His people.

> Will a man rob God? Yet ye have robbed me. But ye say,
> Wherein have we robbed thee? In tithes and offerings.
> (Mal. 3:8)

> Even so hath the Lord ordained that they which preach the
> gospel should live of the gospel. (1 Cor. 9:14)

> Let him that is taught in the word communicate unto him that
> teacheth in all good things. (Gal. 6:6)

The labourer is worthy of his reward. (1 Tim. 5:18*b*)

Had the widow been intimidated by the people in nicer clothing, exuding an air of all's right with the world and depositing abundant coinage, she might have slunk away, embarrassed, with those two small coins held tightly in her hand. Instead she thought in terms of her own individual privilege and responsibility. The fact that she gave everything indicates that her sense of privilege and blessing was uppermost. Wouldn't our giving likewise increase if we made that shift of focus?

In whom we have redemption through his blood, the forgiveness of sins, according to the riches of his grace. (Eph. 1:7)

And the grace of our Lord was exceeding abundant with faith and love which is in Christ Jesus. (1 Tim. 1:14)

For if there be first a willing mind, it is accepted according to that a man hath, and not according to that he hath not. (2 Cor. 8:12)

Then the people rejoiced, for that they offered willingly, because with perfect heart they offered willingly to the Lord. (1 Chron. 29:9*a*)

The "big givers" in the temple that day went home, perhaps, to build grander earthly edifices for themselves. The widow went home having laid up richly in God's eternal kingdom.

Lay not up for yourselves treasures upon earth, where moth and rust doth corrupt, and where thieves break through and steal: but lay up for yourselves treasures in heaven, where neither moth nor rust doth corrupt, and where thieves do not break through nor steal: for where your treasure is, there will your heart be also. (Matt. 6:19–21)

I wonder if the widow's poverty itself was a positive factor in her giving. That is, her own experience living hand-to-mouth made her sensitive to the needs of the priests and their families—those who were dependent upon the gifts of lay people. I believe that an even deeper factor is operative in this dear woman. She had so little of this earth that her heart could be wholly taken up with her God. I marvel in opportunities I've had to meet people in the USA and other countries who exist on incomes that are minimal or even poverty level and yet demonstrate huge generosity toward God's work. What a convicting reality!

Finally, the widow's spirit of supportiveness speaks to me. As a widow, she could have taken up a place in the temple and complained that the religious system wasn't taking proper care of her, that she'd been neglected, missing out on alms distributed by the priests. Not so. Her spirit and behavior were entirely positive.

The widow Jesus highlighted in His day reflects brightly into ours. Poor in money, she was rich in heart. Imagine what the Lord's work—and indeed the world—would be if every one of us were like her. How wonderful if we took to heart the apostle Paul's admonition to "abound in this grace also" (2 Cor. 8: 7–6).

Chapter 16

MARY MAGDALENE

These studies of women whom Jesus met began with one Mary and end with another. Like the Mary who was Jesus' mother, Mary Magdalene has also been the subject of wild imaginings and extra-Scripture embroidery—with much of it having salacious overtones. The Gospels allow us nothing more than tiny peeks here and there. In an attempt to bring this woman more clearly into focus, we necessarily have to employ imagination, but it will be bounded by knowledge of Christ's own character as well as biblical likelihood.

The time when Jesus initially met Mary is mentioned only in passing in Mark 16:9, "Mary Magdalene, out of whom he had cast seven devils," and again in Luke 8:2*b*, "Out of whom went seven devils."

Those references, however, indicate the depth of spiritual darkness from which she came and why she walked so determinedly and faithfully in the light after meeting Jesus.

"Mary" was a much-used name in the first century. In fact, the Gospel writers mention so many Marys it's difficult to distinguish between them. This particular woman's appellation as "Magdalene" comes from the name of the place where she originated. Magdala, also known as Dalmanutha, was a town located about three miles north of Tiberias on the western shore of the Sea of Galilee.

Her family, her childhood, her friends, her social milieu—we know nothing at all about them. But we do know that by the time she crossed paths with Jesus of Nazareth, she was in desperate straits spiritually.

In our day demon possession is rarely even a topic of conversation, much less a reality to be dealt with. In Jesus' time, however, it seems to have been manifest as often as disease, crippling, or blindness. Perhaps its incidence was rife because of Israel's long descent into empty religious formalism and her failure to bear effective testimony to those around her. The cold, dark spiritual atmosphere would have offered evil spirits great opportunity. Even in modern times missionaries working in remote areas of pagan lands see instances of demon possession.

It is sometimes thought today that Mary Magdalene was a prostitute—or even the one who anointed Jesus' feet in the home of the Pharisee. But there is no biblical evidence to support either idea. Instead, it appears that her problem and her need for Jesus' intervention had all to do with the evil spirits that had invaded her body. We don't know how or when the invasion began or how long it had been going on. But she must have been a pathetic, horrifying sight as she moved about under their influence.

In trying to picture what the torturous experience might have meant to her, I think of two other Bible incidents in which Jesus dealt with demon possession. First, there was the demon-possessed man of Gadara. Three of the Gospel writers, Matthew, Mark, and Luke, record the event with slight variation. The passages are Matthew 8:28–32, Mark 5:1–13, and Luke 8:26–39. I'll pull descriptions from all three to help us get a sense of what Mary Magdalene may have endured before Jesus freed her from demonic enslavement. Matthew tells us there were two demonically crazed men; Mark and Luke concentrate on one. Evidently, one of the duo was so much worse than the other that he predominated. The pertinent point, for our consideration of Mary, is the desperate condition of individuals who were indwelt by devils.

Matthew is brief in his telling. He uses almost a shorthand method to describe the strangeness: "There met him two possessed with devils, coming out of the tombs, exceeding fierce" (8:28*b*). Mark gives more detail, helping us to visualize the scene:

Immediately there met him out of the tombs a man with an unclean spirit, who had his dwelling among the tombs; and no man could bind him, no, not with chains: because that he had been often bound with fetters and chains, and the chains had been plucked asunder by him, and the fetters broken in pieces: neither could any man tame him. And always, night and day, he was in the mountains, and in the tombs, crying, and cutting himself with stones. (5:2*b*–5)

And finally, Luke adds his viewpoint:

There met him out of the city a certain man, which had devils long time, and wore no clothes, neither abode in any house, but in the tombs. . . . For oftentimes [the evil spirit] had caught him: and he was kept bound with chains and in fetters; and he brake the bands, and was driven of the devil into the wilderness. (8:27*b*, 29*b*)

The composite picture is horrific, isn't it? Let's dissect the descriptions to get a better idea of the various aspects of demon possession that may also have been present in Mary Magdalene before Jesus healed her.

Socially there was ostracism due to fearsome behavior. All sense of appropriateness and restraint had been destroyed, as evidenced by his nakedness. Mentally the possessed person was strange, irrational, and raving. Physically there was unusual strength. Intentionally there was intense anger and a wish to destroy. Overall living had been reduced to the unthinkable level of animal-like existence.

That list draws us up short when we really think of a human being—and particularly a woman—in such straits. But the story of the Gadarene goes on, and the recorded ultimate effect wrought by the demons clearly shows the depth of satanic darkness with which they imprisoned a person. Jesus Christ demanded the evil spirits to leave their poor, demented human host. The demons besought him to let them inhabit the bodies of a nearby herd of pigs. When He allowed them to do so, the result was astounding:

> And when they were come out, they went into the herd of swine: and, behold, the whole herd of swine ran violently down a steep place into the sea, and perished in the waters" (Matt. 8:32b). "And the unclean spirits went out, and entered into the swine: and the herd ran violently down a steep place into the sea, (they were about two thousand;) and were choked in the sea" (Mark 5:13b). "Then went the devils out of the man, and entered into the swine: and the herd ran violently down a steep place into the lake, and were choked. (Luke 8:33)

How fantastic was the demons' destructiveness—the pigs couldn't stand to be inhabited by them!

Second, and occurring later in Jesus' ministry, another demoniac was healed. His story gives us more insight into a victim's suffering. Matthew 17:15 presented the short version, where he gave the distressed father's plea to Jesus: "Lord, have mercy on my son: for he is lunatick, and sore vexed: for ofttimes he falleth into the fire, and oft into the water." Then came Jesus' response in verse 18: "And Jesus rebuked the devil; and he departed out of him: and the child was cured from that very hour."

Thanks to Mark, the situation takes on much more dimension. We find his presentation of the incident in 9:17–27.

> And one of the multitude answered and said, Master, I have brought unto thee my son, which hath a dumb spirit; and wheresoever he taketh him, he teareth him: and he foameth, and gnasheth with his teeth, and pineth away: and I spake to thy disciples that they should cast him out; and they could not. He answered him, and saith, O faithless generation, how long shall I be with you? how long shall I suffer you? bring him unto me. And they brought him unto him: and when he saw him, straightway the spirit tare him; and he fell on the ground, and wallowed foaming. And he asked his father, How long is it ago since this came unto him? And he said, Of a child. And ofttimes it hath cast him into the fire, and into the waters, to destroy him: but if thou canst do any thing, have compassion on us, and help us. Jesus said unto him, If thou canst believe, all things are possible to him that believeth. And straightway the father of the child cried out, and said with tears, Lord, I believe; help thou mine unbelief. When Jesus saw that the people came running together, he rebuked the foul spirit, saying unto him, Thou dumb and deaf spirit, I charge thee, come out of him, and enter no more into him. And the spirit cried, and rent him sore, and came out of him: and he was as one dead; insomuch that many said, He is dead. But Jesus took him by the hand, and lifted him up; and he arose.

Reading the descriptions of the demonic torments suffered by the boy, I'm sobered to come back to the fact that only one demon was author of it all. That realization has special impact upon our study of Mary Magdalene—who'd been freed from the power of seven demons.

I've often wondered why Mary experienced such an enormous infestation of demons. Maybe she had "invited" them by delving into some of the heathen beliefs and practices around her. Maybe, however, she had lived out the situation Jesus described in one of His sermons, presented in Matthew 12:43–45 and Luke 11:24–26. Since the passages are nearly identical, I'll just quote from Luke.

> When the unclean spirit is gone out of a man, he walketh
> through dry places, seeking rest; and finding none, he saith, I
> will return unto my house whence I came out. And when he
> cometh, he findeth it swept and garnished. Then goeth he, and
> taketh to him seven other spirits more wicked than himself;
> and they enter in, and dwell there: and the last state of that
> man is worse than the first.

Thus Jesus warned against self-reformation and its sure failure. Perhaps that's what Mary had attempted at some point, determinedly ridding herself of one demon and "cleaning house"—only to have multiples join him when he moved back in.

However the demonic indwelling had begun, every moment it continued meant terrific suffering. Considering those seven demons' control of Mary Magdalene, we can be assured that her life before meeting Jesus Christ had been sheer horror.

Evidently, from the moment of her healing Mary of Magdala became one of Jesus' most faithful followers. It was not just that He had given her peace to replace the torment she had known; rather, He was her peace. She wanted always to be near Him, to listen, to learn, and to serve. She was not turned aside from her devotion by distances traveled: "And it came to pass afterward, that he went throughout every city and village, preaching and shewing the glad tidings of the kingdom of God: and the twelve were with him, and certain women, which had been healed of evil spirits and infirmities, Mary called Magdalene . . ." (Luke 8:1–3).

Nor did she become disloyal when her beloved Lord Jesus experienced ever-intensifying enmity. The latter is abundantly evident in the fact of her being at the cross.

> There were also women looking on afar off: among whom was Mary Magdalene. (Mark 15:40)

> And all his acquaintance, and the women that followed him from Galilee, stood afar off, beholding these things. (Luke 23:49)

> Now there stood by the cross of Jesus his mother, and his mother's sister, Mary the wife of Cleophas, and Mary Magdalene. (John 19:25)

Whatever difficulties Mary Magdalene may have experienced in the months of traveling miles on foot, lodging in inconvenient accommodations, providing practical care for the Master and His disciples, and the agony of watching Him die, her dedication was more than rewarded. One of the most beautiful scenes in all the Bible focuses on Mary. The apostle John paints the picture for us in John 20:1–2, then 11–18.

> The first day of the week cometh Mary Magdalene early, when it was yet dark unto the sepulchre, and seeth the stone taken away from the sepulchre. Then she runneth, and cometh to Simon Peter, and to the other disciple whom Jesus loved, and saith unto them, They have taken away the Lord out of the sepulchre, and we know not where they have laid him. . . . But Mary stood without at the sepulchre weeping: and as she wept, she stooped down, and looked into the sepulchre, and seeth two angels in white sitting, the one at the head, and the other at the feet, where the body of Jesus had lain. And they say unto her,

Woman, why weepest thou? She saith unto them, Because they
have taken away my Lord, and I know not where they have laid
him. And when she had thus said, she turned herself back, and
saw Jesus standing, and knew not that it was Jesus. Jesus saith
unto her, Woman, why weepest thou? whom seekest thou? She,
supposing him to be the gardener, saith unto him, Sir, if thou
have borne him hence, tell me where thou hast laid him, and
I will take him away. Jesus saith unto her, Mary. She turned
herself, and saith unto him, Rabboni; which is to say, Master.
Jesus saith unto her, Touch me not; for I am not yet ascended to
my Father: but go to my brethren, and say unto them, I ascend
unto my Father, and your Father; and to my God, and your
God. Mary Magdalene came and told the disciples that she had
seen the Lord, and that he had spoken these things unto her.

Many disciples had avoided visiting the tomb—whether from
exhaustion, discouragement, or fear. Mary Magdalene let none of
those hinder; she was determined to be near that place where the
body of her Lord had been taken. The darkness through which
she made her way that early, early morning was reminiscent of the
dark binding by Satan's demons she had known before Jesus freed
her. And surely the garden seemed even darker when she found
the tomb empty. How could it be? The questions ricocheting
through her mind found no answers, but rather were worsened by
questions posed by others: two white-clad figures in the tomb and
a stranger who came up behind her. Why must she try to answer,
when she was so shocked by the yawning sepulcher, when her
tears were blinding her? But perhaps the gardener could be of help
to her . . . the gardener . . . He . . . He spoke her name! Yet it wasn't
the name spoken but the voice: that well-known, that loved voice . . .
the voice that had bade her inhabiting tormentors flee. It could
only be . . . it was the Master! The radiance of light shining into
Mary's soul banished the garden's shadows, made her tears and

her fears evaporate, made her heart feel that it must burst from gladness. Her blessed Lord Jesus had fulfilled His promise: He had conquered death. As she had done in days before, so now too she heard and heeded. And she, a woman who had been demon-possessed, was first to see the risen Lord, first to know salvation's work had been completed, and first to tell the glorious news: "He is risen!"

*M*eeting Him with Her

Today we may feel a false security in thinking that demonic activity was characteristic only of the distant past. Just the opposite is true. Satan himself and his dark cohorts are unceasingly at work, blinding sinners and bombarding saints. No, we don't recognize or talk of demon possession. But any thoughtful look at the world around us with a Bible in hand makes demonic warfare evident. How else to explain the world at large in its ever-faster plunge into paganism? How else to comprehend the increasing evidences of evil in human thought and behavior? How else to make sense of the church invisible suffering weakness, frivolity, and moral failure in both pew and pulpit? Rather than allowing ourselves to be lulled into complacency, we must become awake and aware: "Be sober, be vigilant; because your adversary the devil, as a roaring lion, walketh about, seeking whom he may devour" (1 Pet. 5:8) and also "knowing the time, that now it is high time to awake out of sleep: for now is our salvation nearer than when we believed" (Rom. 13:11).

Interpreting modernity in the light of Scripture, there is every indication that our sin-cursed planet Earth is nearing its God-determined end. He who acts as the god of this world ever more rabidly opposes the true, sovereign God and seeks to take to destruction with him as many souls as possible.

Satan dangles shiny lures before each of us, promising wonderful things. He paints an innocent landscape, assuring us that it holds indescribable marvels of happiness. But within the lure is a vicious hook, and beneath the innocent-seeming surface of the landscape a cruel trap. Once we have taken the bait or entered the pictured landscape, he would have us think the hook's hold is permanent, and the trap inescapable. Mary Magdalene beautifully illustrates that even someone most tightly bound by Satan's cords can be set free by Jesus Christ. Total, permanent escape comes by Him— and by Him only. As He said in John 8:36, "If the Son therefore shall make you free, ye shall be free indeed."

THERE ARE NO HOPELESS CASES.

There are no hopeless cases. Hebrews 7:25 assures us that "he is able also to save them to the uttermost that come unto God by him, seeing he ever liveth to make intercession for them." And 1 Corinthians 6:9–11 tells us what some of those "uttermosts" may be or may have been.

> Know ye not that the unrighteous shall not inherit the kingdom of God? Be not deceived: neither fornicators, nor idolators, nor adulterers, nor effeminate, nor abusers of themselves with mankind, nor thieves, nor covetous, nor drunkards, nor revilers, nor extortioners, shall inherit the kingdom of God. And such were some of you: but ye are washed, but ye are sanctified,

but ye are justified in the name of the Lord Jesus, and by the Spirit of our God.

Satan and his hordes not only seek to destroy individuals but also carry on intense sabotage within the church. The writers of the New Testament letters to believers posted warning after warning. Soak in the few of those that follow, recognizing every one of them to be current. The warnings were originally addressed to Paul's young pastor friend, Timothy.

Some having swerved have turned aside unto vain jangling; desiring to be teachers of the law; understanding neither what they say, nor whereof they affirm. (1 Tim. 1:6*b*–7)

Now the Spirit speaketh expressly, that in the latter times some shall depart from the faith, giving heed to seducing spirits, and doctrines of devils. (1 Tim. 4:1–2)

If any man teach otherwise, and consent not to wholesome words, even the words of our Lord Jesus Christ, and to the doctrine which is according to godliness; he is proud, knowing nothing, but doting about questions and strifes of words, whereof cometh envy, strife, railings, evil surmisings, perverse disputings of men of corrupt minds, and destitute of the truth, supposing that gain is godliness. (1 Tim. 6:3–5*a*)

For men shall be lovers of their own selves, covetous, boasters, proud, blasphemers, disobedient to parents, unthankful, unholy, without natural affection, trucebreakers, false accusers, incontinent, fierce, despisers of those that are good, traitors, heady, highminded, lovers of pleasures more than lovers of God; having a form of godliness, but denying the power thereof. (2 Tim. 3:2–5*a*)

Twenty-first century churches—fundamental churches— are seeing those fearsome black-and-white descriptions become three-dimensional, full-color reality within their walls. Nor are our churches Satan-plagued only in the pews. He is daily working devastation in the pulpits as well. In fact, in many cases the corruption actually begins in the pulpits. And what happens in a nation's churches plays powerfully into that nation's destruction. William Cowper, a British poet who lived from 1731–1800, poetically painted a grim but accurate church portrait.

Where the Leprosy Begins

When Nations are to perish in their sins,
'Tis in the Church the leprosy begins:
The priest, whose office is, with zeal sincere
To watch the fountain and preserve it clear,
Carelessly nods and sleeps upon the brink,
While others poison what the flock must drink;
Or waking at the call of lust alone,
Infuses lies and errors of his own:
His unsuspecting sheep believe it pure,
And, tainted by the very means of cure,
Catch from each other a contagious spot,
The foul forerunner of a general rot.
Then Truth is hush'd that heresy may preach,
And all is trash that reason cannot reach;
Then God's own image on the soul impress'd
Becomes a mockery and a standing jest;
And Faith, the root whence only can arise
The graces of a life that wins the skies,
Loses at once all value and esteem,
Pronounced by greybeards a pernicious dream;
Then Ceremony leads her bigots forth,
Prepared to fight for shadows of no worth;
While Truth, on which eternal things depend,
Finds not, or hardly finds, a single friend:
As soldiers watch the signal of command,
They learn to bow, to kneel, to sit, to stand;
Happy to fill Religion's vacant place
With hollow form, and gesture, and grimace.

Just as no individual is beyond the reach of God's power to save, neither is the church beyond His power to revive. But, individually and corporately, we must return wholeheartedly to the Word—written and living—praying earnestly for God's cleansing touch.

A mighty challenge reaches out to me from Mary Magdalene. Do we, like her, gratefully remember the mighty, freeing work done on Calvary for our soul, and do we faithfully, lovingly, and wholeheartedly honor the Lord Jesus Christ as our Rabboni—*Master?*

Chapter 17
OVERVIEW

We've visited all the women whose meeting with Jesus God chose to record. We've come close to each and examined her self and her situation with an eye to learning from her. And now we leave them. Each one presents a particular lesson for every woman's ongoing personal relationship with Jesus Christ. Each is beautiful in the most accurate sense of the word.

As we move away, let's just reach out for a parting touch from each one with a concentrated, crystallized impression.

Mary—instant belief and acceptance of God's assignment

Anna—choosing "apartness" with the Lord into old age

Samaritan woman—rejection of dead tradition in favor of the Living Word

Peter's mother-in-law—exercising the capacity to serve

Widow of Nain—speechless wonder at God's power

Sinful anointer—sin's greatness motivating love's outpouring

Woman with an issue of blood—sacrificing a heart's secrecy

Jairus's daughter—persistent parental faith

Canaanite—determined intervention for a child

Woman taken in adultery—receiving God's boundless forgiveness

Mary of Bethany—quietness with Christ amid life's busyness

Martha of Bethany—diligence in working for the Lord and directness in speaking to Him

Bowed-together woman—straightening to uprightness

Salome—replacing ambition with humility and service

Widow with two mites—sacrificing on earth for treasure in heaven

Mary Magdalene—abandoning utter enslavement by sin for utter dedication to Christ

The longer I stayed with each character, the nearer and dearer she became. Not one of the women stands as elevated or gigantic. Rather, the littleness of self and immensity of need point us to the Lord Jesus as He truly is: the high and Holy One, Who inhabits eternity yet bends in love to each one of us, His miniscule girl children. Personal littleness exalting God's greatness is expressed in a lovely childlike poem by Christina Rossetti. I believe she captures the heart expression of anyone who truly meets Jesus Christ.

Dear Lord, Let Me Recount to Thee
Some of the great things Thou hast done
*   For me, even me*
*   Thy little one.*

It was not I that cared for Thee,—
But Thou didst set Thy heart upon
*   Me, even me*
*   Thy little one.*

And therefore was it sweet to Thee
To leave Thy majesty and throne,
*   And grow like me*
*   A Little One.*

Meeting Him

A swaddled Baby on the knee
Of a dear mother of Thine own,
        Quite weak like me
        Thy little one.
. . . .

Jerusalem and Galilee,—
Thy love embraced not those alone,
        But also me
        Thy little one.

Thy unblemished body on the tree
Was bared and broken to atone
        For me, for me
        Thy little one.
. . . .

And love of me arose with Thee
When death and hell lay overthrown:
        Thou lovedst me
        Thy little one.

And love of me went up with Thee
To sit upon Thy Father's throne:
        Thou lovest me
        Thy little one.

Lord, as Thou me, so would I Thee
Love in pure love's communion,
        For thou lov'st me
        Thy little one.

Which love of me bring back with Thee
To judgment when the trump is blown,
        Still loving me
        Thy little one.

STUDY GUIDE

Before Christ came to earth women generally enjoyed little respect. At best they were second-class citizens. He brought them a new level of recognition. He treated them as individuals with valuable contributions. *Meeting Him* presents the Bible scenes in which Jesus dealt with women. In this study guide we'll follow the read-ponder-project approach as we focus on sixteen women who came face to face with the Lord Jesus Christ.

Read—Read the book and the related verses to get the clear message that the Gospel writers wanted us to learn about Jesus' dealings with these women.

Ponder—Look at the passages and others throughout the Bible to consider why these events are important to us today.

Project—Apply the things we've learned.

Chapter 1
MARY, MOTHER OF JESUS
Read chapter 1 from *Meeting Him*.

READ
1. Read Luke 1:26–28. List at least four things we learn about Mary in these verses.

2. In your own words give Mary's response to the angel's proclamation in Luke 1:35–37.

3. Mary was present when Jesus performed His first miracle. Describe the setting and the miracle (John 2:1–11).

4. What other women besides Mary were at Jesus' crucifixion (Matt. 27:55–56; Mark 15:40–41; Luke 23:49; John 19:25)?

PONDER

5. When Elisabeth greeted Mary, Mary responded with what today we call the Magnificat (Luke 1:46–55). This was her public praise to God. She didn't magnify herself but God. List all the attributes of God that she mentions in the Magnificat.

6. The psalms are full of praise to God. What attributes of God are mentioned by the psalmist in the following verses?
   a. Psalm 7:17
   b. Psalm 21:13
   c. Psalm 63:3
   d. Psalm 71:22
   e. Psalm 107:8

7. What is meant by the following sentences from the book concerning Jesus' first miracle? "[Mary] had appealed to [Jesus] for action, for provision in the practical, everyday sense. But from that time on His provision would be spiritual and eternal."

8. In John 19:26–27, what provision did Jesus make for Mary from the cross? What are some things we can learn from His tender care for His mother?

PROJECT

9. Consider Luke 1:38. What should always be our response to the Lord's leading?

10. What one thing about Mary spoke to you most? How will you apply this to your life today?

Chapter 2
ANNA
Read chapter 2 from *Meeting Him*.

READ

1. How does Luke describe Anna in 2:36–37?

2. According to verse 37 how did she serve God in the temple?

3. As Anna came into the temple at the moment of Jesus' dedication (v. 38), in what two ways did she acknowledged His deity?

4. Luke 2:36 describes Anna as a prophetess. How did she fulfill her role as a prophetess according to 2:38?

PONDER

5. From the book we learn that Anna means "grace." How did God show grace to Anna that day in the temple?

6. Based on what the Scriptures say about Anna, how do we know that she had a God-focused heart?

7. What do the following verses say about widows?
   a. Psalm 146:9
   b. Jeremiah 49:11
   c. Zechariah 7:10

8. Why do you think Anna immediately recognized Who Jesus was that day in the temple?

PROJECT

9. Anna had the rare opportunity to look into the face of God that day in the temple, but she also had had a faithful daily focus upward to the face of God most of her adult life. What are some specific ways you can emulate her upward focus today?

10. What one thing about Anna spoke to you most? How will you apply this to your life today?

Chapter 3
THE SAMARITAN WOMAN
Read chapter 3 from *Meeting Him*.

READ

1. John 4:3 says, "And [Jesus] must needs go through Samaria." From what you've read in the book or using a study Bible, describe Samaria in Jesus' day.

2. Read John 4:6–9. Why was it unusual for Jesus to address the Samaritan woman?

3. Read John 4:7–24. The Samaritan woman asked Jesus several questions at the well in Sychar. Rewrite in your own words at least three questions that this woman asked and give Jesus' responses to her.

4. The first words of direct identification of Jesus Himself as Messiah were spoken to this woman. What were they (John 4:25–26)?

PONDER

5. This woman of Samaria initially pointed out the enormous chasm of religious form separating the Jews from the Samaritans. How did Jesus immediately redirect her thoughts to get to the heart of His message to her (John 4:10)?

6. Jesus promised the Samaritan that if she would drink of His living water, she would never thirst again but that the water He offered to her would be a "well of water springing up into everlasting life." What does the Bible say about everlasting life in the following verses?
   a. Daniel 12:1–3
   b. John 3:14–21
   c. Romans 6:20–23

7. Based on Psalm 42:1–2, how should we seek after Christ's living water? Give some practical ways that you can do that today.

8. After the Samaritan woman had recognized and received Jesus as the living water, she left her waterpot and did what? What are some things in your life that hinder you from sharing the gospel with those unsaved people you know personally?

PROJECT

9. "The woman of Sychar spoke of [Christ] so persistently, so convincingly, that others came to see and hear the Man at the well." Choose one of the hindrances you listed in question 8

and describe how you can remove it from your life to make an opportunity to witness to someone close to you this week.

10. What one thing about the Samaritan woman spoke to you most? How will you apply this to your life today?

Chapter 4
PETER'S MOTHER-IN-LAW
Read chapter 4 from *Meeting Him*.

READ

1. According to Mark 1:21–29, where had Jesus and His disciples been immediately before they went to Peter's house in Capernaum?

2. Read again Matthew 8:14–15; Mark 1:29–31; and Luke 4:38–39. What specific details are given in these passages by the Gospel writers about Peter's mother-in-law?

3. Read Isaiah 35:5–6. How does Jesus' encounter with Peter's mother-in-law fulfill this prophecy about Messiah?

4. What did she immediately begin to do after the fever left her (Luke 4:39)?

PONDER

5. Jesus touched Peter's mother-in-law and relieved her fever. What are some other infirmities that Jesus healed with a touch?
   a. Matthew 9:20
   b. Matthew 20:30–34
   c. Mark 1:40–41
   d. Mark 7:32–35

6. In Luke 4:39 Jesus rebuked this woman's fever and it left her. What else did Jesus rebuke, according to Matthew 17:18 and Mark 9:24, and what was the result of the rebuke?

7. Who told Jesus about Peter's mother-in-law's fever? What does this teach us about intercession for others?

8. What was Jesus' direct effect on Peter's mother-in-law? What does her immediate response teach us about what we should be doing for others?

PROJECT

9. Read Galatians 5:13. What is something specific that you can do for someone you know to show love and concern for him or her this week?

10. What one thing about Peter's mother-in-law spoke to you most? How will you apply this to your life today?

Chapter 5
THE WIDOW OF NAIN

Read chapter 5 from *Meeting Him*.

READ

1. Read again Luke 7:11–15. What does Luke tell us about this woman from Nain?

2. Knowing what we do about her, why would her son's death have been a devastating blow to her?

3. The Gospels record that Jesus raised three people from the dead—a child, this young man, and an adult. Who were the other two?

    a. Matthew 9:18–19, 23–25
    b. John 11:32–45

4. Read Exodus 22:22–23. What promise does God give to those who are most needy? As Jesus approached the city of Nain and He and His disciples came upon the funeral procession, how did He show compassion to the grief-stricken widow?

PONDER

5. Luke 7:13 says, "And when the Lord saw her, he had compassion on her." Jesus' compassion that day brought the widow's son back to life. No need escaped His notice. Read the

following passages and note how He compassionately changed others' lives.

    a. Matthew 14:14
    b. Matthew 15:32–39
    c. Mark 1:41–42

6. Read again Luke 7:13. In His omniscience Jesus picked out the grieving widow from the large crowd of mourners. What encouragement can this be to you in a time of need?

7. Jesus met the widow of Nain outside the city on the way to a cemetery. Wherever we are, we have His promise: "And, lo, I am with you alway, even unto the end of the world" (Matt. 28:20). Describe a recent incident in which you clearly felt God's presence with you.

8. How is Matthew 6:8 a constant reminder of God's watchful care over His children?

PROJECT

9. Read Exodus 3:7. When you enter a difficult time, how can this verse bring comfort to your heart?

10. What one thing about the widow of Nain spoke to you most? How will you apply this to your life today?

Chapter 6
THE SINFUL ANOINTER

Read chapter 6 from *Meeting Him*.

READ

1. Read again Luke 7:36–39. Why was this woman out of place and unwelcome in Simon's home?

2. What was Simon's response to this woman? Why do you think he didn't express his thoughts out loud?

3. Although as far as we know the woman did not speak a word to Jesus, how did she express her heartfelt devotion to Him?

4. Based on Luke 7:44–50, what did Jesus offer this woman that was different from what other men had offered her?

PONDER

5. This woman entered Simon's home unbidden and unwelcome. Have you ever allowed people around you to deter you from doing something to honor God? Explain.

6. This woman anointed Jesus with oil from an alabaster box. Read the following verses from the Old Testament. In each case, who was anointed and what was his position in life?
   a. 1 Kings 19:16*b*
   b. Exodus 29:1–7
   c. 1 Kings 1:39

7. In this passage Jesus told the story of two debtors, one who owed little and one who owed much. Compare and contrast Simon and the woman.

8. How had this woman entered Simon's house? How did she leave?

PROJECT

9. When this woman knelt at Jesus' feet, He didn't flinch, pull away, or reprove her. List some ways this can be an encouragement to you today.

10. What one thing about the sinful anointer spoke to you most? How will you apply this to your life today?

Chapter 7
THE WOMAN WITH AN ISSUE OF BLOOD
Read chapter 7 from *Meeting Him*.

READ

1. What specific things does the Bible tell us about this woman with the "issue of blood" (Matt. 9:20; Mark 5:25–26)?

2. What do Mark and Luke tell us about the crowd that was following Jesus (Mark 5:24; Luke 8:42, 45)?

3. Matthew 17:20 says, "If ye have faith as a grain of mustard seed, ye shall say unto this mountain, Remove hence to yonder place; and it shall remove; and nothing shall be impossible unto you." In what two ways did Jesus honor this woman's small faith (Mark 5:29)?

4. Mark says the woman approached Jesus "fearing and trembling . . . and fell down before him." How did Jesus address her? What assurances did He give her?

PONDER

5. Besides the physical "plague" that this woman had suffered for twelve years, according to Mark 5:24–26 and Luke 8:43 what other indignities had she suffered?

6. Read Leviticus 15:19–23. What does this passage say about her condition? As a socially isolated woman, what might have given her courage to seek out Jesus in the crowd (Mark 5:27)?

7. Not everyone who has a chronic illness will be healed. Read the following verses and note why God does not take away all infirmities. What can we learn from them?
   a. Psalm 119:71
   b. Romans 5:3
   c. 2 Corinthians 12:7–9

8. Why do you think Jesus made this woman come forth publicly (Luke 8:47–48; Mark 5:33–34)?

PROJECT

9. The book discusses intimate sins that may plague us as the issue of blood plagued this woman. If we move forward to touch the hem of Christ's garment, He can free us from our intimate maladies of mind and heart. Rewrite Psalm 51:1–12 in your own words and then pray like David and ask God to forgive you of those intimate sins.

10. What one thing about the woman with the issue of blood spoke to you most? How will you apply this to your life today?

Chapter 8
Jairus's Daughter

Read chapter 8 from *Meeting Him*.

Read

1. Read again Mark 5:22 and Luke 8:41. Who was Jairus?

2. Who entered his house with Jesus (Mark 5:37)?

3. What was Jesus' response to the news of the messengers (Matt. 9:24)?

4. What was His response to Jairus (Mark 5:36)?

Ponder

5. How was Jairus different from the woman with the issue of blood?

6. Why do you think Jesus said the girl was asleep (Matt. 9:24; Mark 5:39; Luke 8:53)?

7. Jesus selected Peter, James, and John to witness Jairus's daughter's being raised from the dead. At what other events were these three disciples the only witnesses?
   a. Mark 9:2
   b. Mark 14:33

8. What delayed Jesus from going to Jairus's home (Mark 5:24–35)? What about this delay demonstrated Jesus' power in a greater way (Mark 5:22–23, 35–42)?

Project

9. Jesus told Jairus, "Be not afraid, only believe." Find three verses on fear and faith that you can use when you face your next difficulty or challenge. Give the references.

10. What one thing about the incident with Jairus's daughter spoke to you most? How will you apply this to your life today?

Chapter 9
The Canaanite Woman

Read chapter 9 from *Meeting Him*.

Read

1. Read Matthew 15:1–20. What three groups did Jesus address before the incident with the Canaanite woman?

2. How did she address Jesus (Matt. 15:22)? What did she acknowledge by the title she used for Him?

3. According to Matthew 15:23, what was Jesus' initial response to this woman's request?

4. Read again Matthew 15:12–16. How do we know that this woman had greater faith than the Jews mentioned earlier in the chapter?

Ponder

5. Why do you think Jesus wanted to go to Tyre and Sidon?

6. Jesus told her, "Let the children first be filled." Who were the children He was referring to, and what in that statement encouraged her to continue to plead for her daughter?

7. How did this woman show her humility before Jesus?
   a. Matthew 15:25*a*
   b. Matthew 15:25*b*
   c. Matthew 15:27

8. This woman was a Canaanite, or Syrophenician—a Gentile. How is Jesus' response to her plea for her daughter—"O woman, great is thy faith: be it unto thee even as thou wilt"— a fulfillment of Genesis 12:3?

Project

9. This story of the Syrophenician woman illustrates that grace would be given to all people. She was a foreigner, she was an outsider, and she was an intrusion on Jesus' time out of the limelight. How has Jesus' response to her encouraged you to make time for those needy people around you?

10. What one thing about the Canaanite woman spoke to you most? How will you apply this to your life today?

Chapter 10
The Woman Taken in Adultery
Read chapter 10 from *Meeting Him*.

Read

1. Why had Jesus come to the temple (John 8:2)?

2. According to Leviticus 20:10 and Deuteronomy 22:22, were the men following the law fully in bringing the woman to Jesus? Why or why not?

3. Although Jesus didn't respond to the men as they had hoped, how did He show that He recognized the woman's sin (John 8:11)?

4. The Scripture makes clear that sins of the spirit are as heinous to God as are sins of the flesh. List some sins of the spirit that Jesus taught against in the Sermon on the Mount (Matt. 5:21–28).

Ponder

5. According to John 8:6, what was the real reason that the men brought the woman taken in adultery to Jesus?

6. This woman's accusers considered themselves greatly superior to her. What did their leaving indicate?

7. What effect did Jesus' statement "He that is without sin among you, let him first cast a stone at her" have on this woman's accusers?

8. Who could have thrown the first stone? What do these verses say about Jesus?
   a. 2 Corinthians 5:21
   b. Hebrews 9:14
   c. 1 Peter 2:22

PROJECT

9. How should we respond to public sin (e.g., John 7:24; Gal. 6:1–2)?

10. What one thing about the woman taken in adultery spoke to you most? How will you apply this to your life today?

Chapter 11
MARY OF BETHANY

Read chapter 11 from *Meeting Him*.

READ

1. In what three locations do we meet Mary in the Scriptures (Luke 10:38–40; John 11:28–31; Matt. 26:6–13)?

2. What was Mary doing in these instances above?

3. Who, according to John, objected to Mary's anointing Jesus with the spikenard (12:4)? Why did he object (12:6)?

4. Why, according to Jesus, was this anointing appropriate (Matt. 26:10–12)?

PONDER

5. Although Jesus didn't say that Martha's physical activity of serving was unimportant, what did He say about the activity Mary had chosen? What does this say about women studying the Scriptures?

6. Jesus responded with tears when He saw Mary's anguished grief over her brother's death. What else do the following verses teach us about Jesus and His sharing our hurts?
   a. Matthew 6:7–8
   b. Hebrews 4:15–16

7. Mary sacrificed something of great value to honor the Lord and was criticized for it. What was her response? What should be our response according to Matthew 5:11–12?

8. Jesus said of Mary, "This also that she hath done shall be spoken of for a memorial of her." How is Mary still having an impact on women today?

Project
9. What are some of the "many things" you may be anxious about that you can lay aside today so that you will have more time to seek the "one needful thing" that Mary chose?

10. What one thing about Mary spoke to you most? How will you apply this to your life today?

Chapter 12
Martha of Bethany
Read chapter 12 from *Meeting Him.*

Read
1. In what three locations do we meet Martha in the Scriptures (Luke 10:38–40; John 11:28–35; 12:2)?

2. What was Martha doing in each of the instances above?

3. When Jesus told Martha, "I am the resurrection, and the life," what two things did she affirm about Him (John 11:27)?

4. According to Jesus' own words, what was the purpose of the miracle at Lazarus's tomb (Luke 11:4, 40)?

Ponder
5. Jesus didn't diminish the importance of Martha's service to Him and His disciples. What did He gently chide her for?

6. When Martha voiced her irritation with Mary for doing all the work in serving Jesus and His disciples, Jesus contrasted the "many things" she was doing with the "one needful thing." What was that needful thing?

7. When Martha told Jesus she knew that Lazarus would rise again, she obviously knew what the Jews taught about

resurrection and may also have been referring to Jesus' earlier teachings. Read the following verses and note what He had said about a resurrection of believers "at the last day."

    a. John 5:21, 25–29
    b. John 6:39–44

8. Although Martha stated that she believed Jesus could raise her brother from the dead, how do we know that she wasn't totally convinced (John 11:39–40)?

PROJECT

9. Describe a time in which you were resentful or stressed out in your service for the Lord. How should you have handled the situation differently?

10. What one thing about Martha spoke to you most? How will you apply this to your life today?

Chapter 13
THE BOWED-TOGETHER WOMAN
Read chapter 13 from *Meeting Him*.

READ

1. What was the woman's infirmity and how long had she suffered from it?

2. The woman with the issue of blood came up behind Jesus and touched His garment. How was this bowed-together woman's experience with meeting Jesus different (Luke 13:12–13)?

3. What was her immediate response to being healed of her infirmity (Luke 13:13)?

4. When Jesus was criticized for her healing by the ruler of the synagogue, why did He call the man a hypocrite?

PONDER

5. Why do you think this woman was in the synagogue that day (Luke 13:10)?

6. Luke 13:11 says of this woman, "[She] could in no wise lift up herself." How in a spiritual sense is this true of all of us?

7. The ruler of the synagogue was angry that Jesus had healed this woman on the Sabbath. Who else did Jesus heal on the Sabbath?

    a. Matthew 12:10–13

    b. Mark 1:21–28

    c. Luke 14:1–6

    d. John 5:1–9

8. Why do you think the religious leaders responded with anger to this woman's being healed from her long-term infirmity (Luke 13:17)?

PROJECT

9. This woman did not ask Jesus for help. He saw her need and responded. Can you think of several people you know who may need help today? Choose one and describe how you plan to help him or her as soon as it is possible for you to do so.

10. What one thing about the bowed-together woman spoke to you most? How will you apply this to your life today?

Chapter 14
THE MOTHER OF JAMES AND JOHN

Read chapter 14 in *Meeting Him*.

READ

1. Read Matthew 4:21, Mark 1:19–20, and Luke 5:10–11. List three things these verses tell us about Zebedee, Salome's husband.

2. What request did Salome make of the Lord (Matt. 20:20–21)?

3. Jesus addressed His response to her question to her sons. What was His answer to them (Matthew 20:22–23)?

4. Salome was one of the first people to learn of the resurrection. Describe in your own words the event at the tomb (Mark 16:1–8).

PONDER

5. According to the passages above (Matt. 4:21; Mark 1:19–20; Luke 5:10–11) and Mark 15:40–41, how do we know that Zebedee's family fully supported Jesus in His ministry?

6. When Jesus asked Salome's sons if they could drink of the cup that He would drink of, He told them they would indeed drink of the same cup of suffering. How was Jesus' statement fulfilled in each of their lives?

   a. Acts 12:2
   b. Revelation 1:9

7. Whom did Jesus say would determine who would have the places of prominence on His right hand and left hand (Matt. 20:23; Mark 10:40)?

8. Of the disciples, John is the only one named as having been present at the crucifixion. In this instance, the women who followed Jesus seemed to have been more courageous to show their devotion to Him while He was on the cross. Who of His followers are also mentioned as being present (Matt. 27:55–56; Mark 15:40; Luke 23:49)?

PROJECT

9. Salome and the other women who heard the angel's declaration at the empty tomb were frightened, but they did what he told them to do (Matt. 28:8). Are you afraid to witness for the Lord or to take a stand for Him? Their willing response can encourage you to overcome your fear to obey His commands. List some things you've been afraid to do in the past. Pray for courage to follow His commands in spite of your fears.

10. What one thing about James and John's mother spoke to you most? How will you apply this to your life today?

Chapter 15
WOMAN WITH TWO MITES
Read chapter 15 in *Meeting Him*.

READ

1. Where was Jesus when He saw the woman in this story (Mark 12:41)?

2. How did Mark describe her (Mark 12:42)?

3. What is a mite?

4. How much had this woman given?

PONDER

5. How does the Bible contrast this woman with the Jewish leaders in the temple (Mark 12:38–42)?

6. What did Jesus mean when He told His disciples that this woman had given more than all the rich people around her?

7. What does Jesus say about treasure in the following verses?
   a. Matthew 6:19–21
   b. Luke 12:15–21

8. What does Matthew 6:31–33 say about God's providing for our needs?

PROJECT

9. Read 2 Corinthians 8:1–5. Describe a time recently that you had the opportunity to give in a sacrificial way. Did you?

10. What one thing about the widow with two mites spoke to you most? How will you apply this to your life today?

Chapter 16
MARY MAGDALENE
Read chapter 16 in *Meeting Him*.

READ
1. Where was this Mary from?

2. Mary was a faithful follower and supporter of Jesus. What had He delivered her from?

3. The first time Mary is mentioned, what was she doing (Luke 8:1–3)?

4. When Mary saw Jesus in the garden on the resurrection morning, what special task did He give her (John 20:17)?

PONDER
5. According to Luke 8:1–3 and Mark 15:41, how was Jesus and His disciples' ministry supported and promoted?

6. Mary is one of the few people mentioned who witnessed many of the events surrounding the crucifixion? What specific events was she present at?
   a. John 19:25
   b. Matthew 27:57–61
   c. Mark 16:9

7. Angels announced Jesus' conception to Mary (Luke 1:30–33) and His resurrection to Mary Magdalene (Matt. 28:1–7). Write out these two angelic announcements in your own words.

8. Why do you think Mary was the first person whom Jesus appeared to after the resurrection (Mark 16:9)?

PROJECT
9. Mary was asked to share the good news of the resurrection (Mark 16:10; John 20:18). If you have not already done so, write out in the front of your Bible or on a small card salvation verses you can share with lost men and women around you.

10. What one thing about Mary Magdalene spoke to you most? How will you apply this to your life today?